WHY IS THERE A
MENORAH
ON THE ALTAR?

WHY IS THERE A
MENORAH
ON THE ALTAR?

Jewish Roots
of Christian Worship

MEREDITH GOULD, Ph.D.

Seabury Books
NEW YORK

Unless otherwise noted, the Scripture quotations contained herein are from the New Revised Standard Version Bible, copyright © 1989 by the Division of Christian Education of the National Council of Churches of Christ in the U.S.A. Used by permission. All rights reserved.

Cover art courtesy of iStockphoto
Cover design by Christina Hope
Page design and typesetting by Beth Oberholtzer

Library of Congress Cataloging-in-Publication Data
  Gould, Meredith, 1951–
    Why is there a Menorah on the altar? Jewish roots of Christian worship / Meredith Gould.
      p. cm.
    Includes bibliographical references and index.
    ISBN 978-1-59627-117-3 (pbk.)
  1. Public worship. 2. Spiritual life. 3. Christianity—Origin. 4. Judaism—History—To 70 A.D. 5. Judaism—Influence. 6. Judaism—Relations—Christianity. 7. Christianity and other religions—Judaism. I. Title.
BV10.3.G68 2009
261.2'6—dc22

                                                        2009019666

Seabury Books
445 Fifth Avenue
New York, New York 10016

www.seaburybooks.com

An imprint of Church Publishing Incorporated

5 4 3 2 1

For Father Marty O'Brien and Bruce Reim,
men of abiding faith and wise counsel
whose encouragement made this book possible.

Contents

Acknowledgments

Book writing is a solo activity that paradoxically includes lots of people, some in the foreground, some in the background, others of blessed memory. And because I became actively engaged on LinkedIn, Twitter, and Facebook while working on this book, the number of people offering valued support now runs into the hundreds. Hyperbole? Well, I count as supportive anyone who took the time to post an expression of encouragement, even if it was at or under 140 characters! In my world of social media, brevity has delivered wit, witness, and unexpected love, all of which I've received with unexpected delight.

In real life, such as it is, I continue to be the grateful recipient of loving encouragement from friends. For their high tolerance for my authorial snits, I thank: Mark K. Barnes, Barbara Calvanelli, Sharon Grosfeld, Ruth Harrigan (also a first reader), Linda S. Hatt, Deacon Jim Knipper, Kristen West McGuire, Kathleen Ogle, Marion Reinson, Melanie Rigney, Reverend Tim Schenck, and Reverend Daniel J. Webster. Very special thanks to Pat Lorenz who, without batting an eye (perhaps because she was too busy rolling them), generated a list of possible book titles including this winner, *Why Is There a Menorah on the Altar?*

I was fortunate to have people of deep faith, rigorous scholarship, and active religious practice, both Christian and Jewish, comment on the manuscript all along the way. For their generous input, I thank: Lori Brower Albanese, J.C.L., Maureen and Paul Flanagan, P. Griffith Lindell, Jane and Deacon Joe Kupin (who, in addition to providing general feedback, actually verified every scripture citation), and Bruce Reim. Thanks to various manufacturers of buspirone, fluoxetine, and ranitidine, I was able to regard readers' corrections and suggestions with relative aplomb. I am, of course, responsible for whatever errors or interpretative weirdness you discover in the final text.

I make no apology for what may seem like an occasional lapse into apologetics. In fact, my most heartfelt thanks go to Reverend Monsignor Martin O'Brien and Bruce Reim, both of whom have spent years prayerfully shoving me in the direction of writing about the Jewish roots of Christian worship for "regular people."

My mother is to be thanked and praised for sending me texts, some long out of print, from her library of Judaica. She and her partner, Ken Ayers, also tolerated an outrageous level of daughterly neglect by me while I was working on this thing.

For shepherding this book through the editorial process, I thank ever-patient and good-humored Nancy Fitzgerald. For moving everything forward, I appreciate Davis Perkins of Church Publishing Inc. and Joan Castagnone, as well as Ryan Masteller for his work with a production team that included Jennifer Hackett, Christina Hope, and Beth Oberholtzer.

Always and forever, thanks be to God.

Foreword

But for me it is good to be near God;
I have made the Lord God my refuge . . .

PSALM 73:28

My mother used to characterize me as a gastronomic Jew. "You're in it for the food," she'd say. Yes, I'll admit food helped shape my Jewish identity, but so did other aspects of *yiddishkeit* (Jewishness), such as my tendency for ironic self-effacing humor and passion for learning.

Being Jewish also meant having a religious identity shaped by observing holidays and holy days, regular synagogue attendance, and home-based rituals. All of it—culture and religion—mattered, especially because I grew up in the confines of suburban northern New Jersey during a time when anti-Semitism was blatant and acceptable. *Gentleman's Agreement*, Laura Z. Hobson's novel about modern American anti-Semitism, was the first "adult" book my parents allowed me to read; I was in fifth grade. I was in junior high school when Tom Lehrer wrote and sang, "National Brotherhood Week,"[1] which included the rueful big-laugh line, "And everybody hates the Jews." This, too, shaped my identity as a Jew and, as I'd discover, future interactions with other Jews about my embrace of Christianity.

Generally speaking, personal conversations about my cultural and religious identity do not go particularly well. Ask me what I am and brace yourself for what happens next. I'll tell you that I consider myself a Jew in identity, a Christian in faith, and a Catholic in religious practice. Jews tend to find this troubling; Christians seem to find it confusing. Both Christians and Jews usually ask when I converted from Judaism and then wonder why I resist characterizing my call to Catholic Christianity a conversion. I certainly do not consider it a "completion." Depending on the circumstances, I'll either launch into my "once a Jew, always a Jew" soliloquy or quote a few scripture verses about God's faithfulness to his people.

I'm offended whenever one of my Christian brothers or sisters says anything like, "welcome home." Although I'll be sorely tempted to explain how "we" were here first, I'll stop myself. As someone raised Jewish, I understand all too well the dangers of us-them dichotomies. As someone raised Jewish, I am called to *tikkun olam* (repair the world). We are all God's creation and beloved.

My mood will dictate how emphatically I choose to remind you that the one we claim as Lord and Savior lived his earthly life as a Jew and was murdered—by Roman authorities and not "the Jews"—for a variety of reasons. I'll probably add that his name wasn't "Jesus" and his last name wasn't "Christ." Then, to lighten up the conversation, I'll say I have a multiple spirituality disorder. Hilarious, right? I've been doing this shtick for years to explain how being baptized did not—could not—eradicate my Jewish identity. I cannot help but see Christianity through Jewish eyes and why would I?

If anything, worshipping at a liturgical church has enhanced my gratitude for years of Jewish education and synagogue attendance. Studying the two thousand years of Jewish history pre-dating Jesus' birth has helped me appreciate the structure and content of Christian liturgy as well as the sacraments of Baptism and Holy Communion. It has helped me understand how Confirmation could sometimes be characterized as a "sacrament in search of a theology." And it certainly enhances my worship experience each and every time I participate in liturgy—either from the pews as a congregant, from the loft as a choir member, or from the ambo as a lector.

In this book, I identify the Jewish roots of what are sometimes incorrectly perceived by well-meaning Christians as uniquely Christian artifacts and practices within today's liturgical churches (Roman Catholic, Lutheran, Episcopal). Working within the Jewish tradition of *midrash*, I use scripture as well as historical events up to and through the first century to illustrate Judaism's enduring legacy even after Christianity became a separate religion. I've taken this approach hoping to reveal how, in so many important ways, Christians and Jews are more alike than we are different. I believe that living in the respectful knowledge of our shared heritage is one way to begin repairing the shattered world of Christian-Jewish relations. I believe with all my heart, mind, and spirit that this healing work is something we are all called to, no matter what our religious affiliation.

3 Adar 5769
First Week of Lent, 2009

What has been is what will be,
and what has been done is what will be done;

there is nothing new under the sun.
Is there a thing of which it is said,

"See, this is new"? It has already been,
in the ages before us.

ECCLESIASTES 1:9–10

CHAPTER ONE

Reading Scripture

*Your word is a lamp to my feet
and a light to my path.*

PSALM 119:105

If you've picked up this book, it's probably because the title has piqued your curiosity about the "Judeo" part of your Judeo-Christian heritage and you want to learn more about it. To gear up for this adventure, you'll need to hunker down and read quite a bit of scripture. Promise: this will enhance your appreciation of . . . everything! Here, I'll not only suggest *what* to read but *how* to read it. Your response to my counsel will undoubtedly be shaped by the Christian tradition in which you've been raised.

If you're a Roman Catholic, an invitation to read scripture on your own might make you feel a bit nervous at first. Although generations of Catholics read missals while the Mass was being celebrated, only relatively recently have in-the-pew Catholics become as engaged in scripture study as their Protestant sisters and brothers. I can think of a number of esoteric and practical reasons why.

Back in the thirteenth century, laity were flat-out forbidden to read scripture. Proclaiming the word of God and the privilege of interpreting text became the exclusive right of clergy. In part this had to do with literacy levels within the general population; in part it had to do with the clericalism Protestant reformers railed against. While scripture had long been translated from Hebrew into Greek and then into Latin, it wasn't available in the vernacular to literate laity until the sixteenth and seventeenth centuries—for Protestants.

Celebrating the Mass in local languages after the Second Vatican Council (1962–1965) made scripture much more accessible. By the end of the twentieth century, Catholic laity had become more engaged not only with liturgical activities, but also with running parish ministries. This served to generate an increased demand for Bible study. In addition, converts from traditions anchored in scripture study were unwilling to relinquish that upon becoming Catholic. Today, many more regular in-and-out-of-the-pew Catholics read and study Christian scripture on their own or within parish-based groups. But for cradle Catholics of a certain generation, the suggestion that anyone might independently study, interpret, and understand scripture may be off-putting.

If you're a Protestant, an invitation to pay close attention to scripture may seem like no big deal because you've been doing it forever. You, however, might start feeling nervous when you encounter my suggestions about *how* to read scripture, especially if you were raised to view scripture as literal, rather than metaphorical.

So which books of the Bible will help you better understand the subject matter of this book?

The Bible According to . . .

Jews　　　Torah = The Five Books of Moses = The Law

　　　　　　Tanakh = The Five Books of Moses & The Prophets & The Writings

Christians　The Bible = Old Testament & New Testament

　　　　　　The Pentateuch = The Five Books of Moses

But wait! Books of the Bible are arranged differently for Christians and Jews. Plus, there are the Apocryphal/ Deuterocanonical Books of scripture written primarily in Greek, only some of which appear in the Roman Catholic canon—and none in the Protestant canon. What, pray tell, is Hebrew scripture? No, it's not scripture written exclusively in Hebrew, it's what you probably call the "Old Testament" and what I tend to call "Hebrew scripture" because of the distinction proposed by Pope John Paul II. He suggested using the terms "Hebrew scripture" and "Christian scripture" to eliminate the implication that the Tanakh was somehow rendered obsolete by the birth, death, and resurrection of Jesus Christ. Just so you know, some Jews might be offended by the term "Old Testament," while others won't bother making this distinction. In any event, given the power of language, I consider the late pontiff's point worth contemplating, if not embracing in practice.

Which Scripture to Read

I'm exceedingly fond of saying that no Christian can possibly understand how radical Jesus was without reading the Pentateuch—the Five Books of Moses.

As Christians, we believe that God became man and that man was Jesus of Nazareth. Jesus was born a Jew in a particular time and place. He spoke in terms of, and with reference to, the Torah. Like other teachers influenced by the Pharisees, Jesus posed questions, told stories, engaged in lively conversation, and at times became exasperated with his students. While gospel stories reveal how his disciples were generally slow to grasp what he was saying, that didn't stop Jesus from using Hebrew scripture as the context and content of his lessons. You'll need to read at least some of this material. And unless you learned Hebrew during Sunday school at Holy Redeemer of Gentiles Church, you'll read scripture in translation. I'll get to translation issues further on in this chapter.

Within the Pentateuch, Leviticus, Numbers, and Deuteronomy are especially important because they spell out the Law of Moses presented in Exodus. There's a lot more to Jewish law than the Decalogue (Ten Commandments), and these books reveal the other 603. That's right, there are 613 *mitzvot* (commandments) that shape the eternal and internal rhythms of Jewish spiritual life. If you can read only one of these three books, I recommend beginning with Deuteronomy because it recapitulates much of what's in Leviticus and Numbers. But please make time to read Leviticus and Numbers, they're fascinating. These books will help you understand the origins of Christian rituals having to do with purification and initiation discussed in Chapter 3 (Worship) and Chapter 4 (Baptism).

Plan to read Genesis and Exodus sooner rather than later. In fact, start there! Whenever anyone asks me where to begin reading the Bible, I always answer the same way: "With Genesis." This always produces a smile and sometimes gets a laugh—but I don't make this recommendation to be clever or artful with scripture. I recommend beginning at the beginning with Genesis for a slew of reasons, including the fact that every possible instance of human bad behavior can be found in this first book of holy scripture. In addition to mapping out the story of creation and the earliest history of the ancient Israelites, Genesis is so filled with crime, passion, sex, intrigue, betrayal, incest, murder, mayhem, gore, vengeance, and violence that most of it is suitable reading for adults only. Reading Genesis should also help you appreciate the derivative nature of soap operas.

Exodus reveals the significance of what biblical scholars and theologians term the "Sinai Event"—when God chose the Israelites "by trials, by signs and wonders, by war, by a mighty hand and an outstretched arm, and by terrifying displays of power" (Deuteronomy 4:34) and gave the Jews an identity and commandments for living. Exodus is a book about God's personal, intimate, and durable relationship with his chosen people.

Reading Exodus should help you understand why contemporary Jews who engage in Christian-Jewish dialogue emphatically reject any theology that suggests Almighty God would ever replace, supersede, nullify, or otherwise break this covenant: ". . . you shall be my treasured possession out of all the peoples. Indeed, the whole earth is mine, but you shall be for me a priestly kingdom and a holy nation" (Exodus 19:5–6). Exodus will also help you appreciate how being Jewish is a complex amalgam of identities. Is it a national identity or a religion? Social scientists include common ancestry and shared culture in their definitions of ethnicity, so is being Jewish an ethnicity? Most Jews would agree that being Jewish is all these things—and then have lots to say about those Jews who might view it differently.[2] Exodus (and certainly parts of

Genesis) also illuminates why bread, water, and blood are such a big sacred deal for Jews and Christians alike, something discussed further in Chapter 5 (Holy Communion).

Managing Multiple Identities

Although it's difficult to separate ethnicity and religion, that doesn't stop some contemporary Jews from embracing the culture and rejecting religious practices. These distinctions are never all that clear-cut. Synagogue attendance on Rosh Hashanah and Yom Kippur is like church attendance on Christmas and Easter. Many secular Jews attend the former; nominally religious Christians attend the latter; both have a robust number of atheists and agnostics in their ranks.

Do Christians have a cultural identity? Although most would argue Christianity is exclusively a religious identity, it's somewhat easy to identify cultural as well as liturgical differences among Roman Catholics, Eastern Orthodox, Lutherans, and Episcopalians. These differences within and between Christian communions tend to be revealed in things such as food and worship styles.

What's that? Have I read the Pentateuch? Yes, but don't ask me to recite chapter and verse. I can, however, usually reel off most of the plagues foisted upon the Egyptians in Exodus, but not necessarily in order and only within the context of a Passover Seder (Exodus 7–11).

Within Christian scripture, please read Luke's gospel as well as Acts of the Apostles, the history of Christianity emerging and separating from Judaism. Both were written after key events changed the religious landscape for Jewish followers of Jesus, events discussed in more detail within the next chapter.

Here I'll simply point out that by the time these books were completed, Jewish and Gentile followers of Jesus were increasingly viewing themselves as a separate sect. Reading both books will help you understand why some Jews started following Jesus of Nazareth and came to accept him as the Christ. Acts of the Apostles will help you understand why the Pharisee who became known as Paul the Apostle focused on Gentiles as he preached Jesus as Christ.[3] Paul's letter to the community in Galatia illuminates key disputes between him and the apostle Peter.

You should probably also read the letter to the Hebrews, even though biblical scholars have identified a number of ways it's problematic: no clear authorship; disputes about when it was written; and whether it's a sermon, a letter, an exhortation to take action, or midrash (i.e., a type of homiletic literature and biblical exegesis or interpretation). Biblical scholars are also divided over whether Hebrews was written to Jewish followers of Jesus, Gentile followers of Jesus, or both.

The issue about who actually wrote what you're reading is also something to remember whenever you read Paul's letters. Biblical scholars agree that while Paul wrote 1 Thessalonians, Galatians, 1 and 2 Corinthians, Romans, Philippians, and Philemon, the rest of his letters were probably written by others.[4] Biblical scholars are debating among themselves when each contribution to Christian scripture was probably written, yet another factor to consider as you read, thus begging the question about how to read these materials most effectively.

Scripture According to . . .

Although everyone trained in the following disciplines works with religious texts, their perspectives differ. In fact, it's not unusual for scholars in one discipline to be unaware of scholars in another. And although there are some who welcome interdisciplinary exchange, it's also not unusual for scholars in one discipline to dismiss scholars in another as misguided or just plain wrong—with no shortage of vitriol, I might note.

Add to the mix authors without academic training who write about religion, God, and scripture. Another category includes authors trained as scholars, but not directly in religion, scripture, or theology, who write about it anyway. I've stumbled into that last category. I believe my academic training as a sociologist happens to be perfect for sorting through the multiple layers of meaning generated by everyone else on this list:

Biblical scholars (exegetes)	Study scripture from numerous perspectives
Theologians	Study God from a religious perspective
Religious Studies scholars	Study religion from a secular perspective

What about clergy and religious? Some are theologians as well as biblical scholars; others are neither; all are in the business of promoting God and scripture from a particular religious perspective. You need to know who works with which agenda.

How to Read Scripture

I'm making several assumptions as I write, and my basic one is that you're someone who likes to read about faith and religion. Your education includes all, some, or none of the following: 1) Scripture study that includes either or both Hebrew and Christian scripture; 2) religious formation (i.e., catechesis) that's either current, vaguely remembered, or long forgotten, possibly rigorous but probably not; and 3) undergraduate work that includes basic courses in the humanities (e.g. the arts, history, languages, literature, philosophy) and social sciences (e.g., anthropology, economics, sociology, political science). Perhaps you have graduate work to your credit, but hopefully not so much that you believe only academicians are capable of interpreting and forming opinions about what they read. No matter what your background, you have an opinion about the meaning and use of scripture shaped by all the above. You do not have to be a biblical scholar, theologian, or cleric to read and interpret scripture, any more than you need to be all or any of these to be a person of faith or to claim religious affiliation. You do, however, take on certain obligations and responsibilities whenever you read scripture.

How should you read scripture? In a word, *critically*.

As a practical matter, this means constantly and consciously asking analytical questions such as, "What's going on?" and then following up with, "Says who?" and "Why?" You do not—should not—forfeit faith by asking these questions. Understanding that scripture has shape-shifted as it has been written, translated, rewritten, and retranslated over the centuries should not undermine your belief that it's the inspired word of God. Understanding that the canon (i.e., the officially recognized set of sacred books) emerged as a result of political wrangling among the men who structured and restructured the church should not undermine your belief that the *ruach hakodesh* (Holy Spirit of God) is ever-present.

I recommend reading scripture with a sense of discovery and curiosity, especially if you come from a religious tradition that discourages challenges from regular folk. You need to know that Judaism has always encouraged critical inquiry. The enduring glory of Judaism is that any Jew may challenge, question, argue, dispute, and refute if verbal jousting leads to more clarity about the Law and *tzedakah* (right relationship with God, all things, and all people).

During the first century, *Bet Hillel* (House of Hillel) and *Bet Shammai* (House of Shammai), schools of Torah interpretation, were so antagonistic that, depending on which authority you read, at least three and as many as five of their disputes are mentioned in the Talmud (Torah commentaries, first oral and later codified in writing). The incidence of dispute between Hillel's and Shammai's disciples was such that this saying emerged: "The one Law has become two laws."[5] Consider the possibility that at least some percentage of the gospel stories featuring Jesus being challenged were not about the Pharisees trapping and tricking Jesus but instead testing his mettle as a teacher and interpreter of the Law. Read those stories more closely and notice how Jesus, good Jew that he is, tests and challenges their interpretations of the Law.

In addition to written Law (Torah), Judaism is shaped by the *Mishnah* (a compendium of legal materials dating ca. 200 C.E.) and the oral tradition of *midrash* (interpretations). For Jews, there's always more to be revealed through study, prayer, and critical inquiry. Hebrew scripture is filled with stories about the Israelites arguing with one another and with God. God commiserates with Moses, calling the Israelites a "stiff-necked people" (Exodus 32:9; 33:5). Moses complains about the complaining, has a temper tantrum, and forfeits his right to enter the land that was promised (Numbers 20:2–13; Deuteronomy 32:48–52). During the first century, Stephen capped his survey of this lively history by characterizing priests of the Sanhedrin as "stiff-necked people . . . just like your fathers" (Acts 7:1–53). He could have used the term "feisty" had the word existed.

Although Christian history is filled with examples of people burned at the stake or otherwise tortured for such temerity, consider taking comfort in knowing that asking tough questions about righteous living is not a sure sign of disobedience. Although it might not seem too attractive considering the consequences of doing so throughout history, you might embrace your Jewish heritage by asking challenging questions while reading scripture. Stephen, in fact, is claimed by the church as its first martyr for being a feisty Jewish follower of Jesus as the Christ (Acts 7:57–59; 8:1).

You can and may read scripture in a variety of ways (e.g., allegorically, historically, as poetry, literary narrative, or mystical code). All these approaches or methods have validity; you simply need to acknowledge if and when you're reading scripture as if it's metaphor, a factual account of events, or a collection of stories and poetry. Notice if and how your understanding and appreciation of scripture changes as you shift reading styles. Being open to reading scripture in a variety of ways will put you right in the mainstream of current efforts to bridge what is increasingly being viewed as a false division between theology and exegesis. During his talk at the 2008 Synod of Catholic Bishops, Anglican bishop and Christian scripture scholar N. T. Wright noted that reading scripture should involve "the heart (*lectio divina*, liturgical reading); the mind (historical/critical study); the soul (church life, tradition, teaching); and strength (mission, kingdom of God)."[6]

What's Faith Got To Do With It?

What about faith? Don't we believe that the Bible is the Word of God and, as Christians, that Jesus was the Word made flesh? How can we reconcile these beliefs with historical critical methodologies for reading text and whatever archaeological research has unearthed? Both Christian and Jewish fundamentalists believe scripture is the inerrant Word of God. Orthodox Jews maintain that God dictated the Torah to Moses, letter-by-letter, and the Talmud lists twenty factors that determine whether Torah scrolls, always painstakingly copied by hand, are "kosher."

Reading critically does not mean jettisoning faith. Many people of faith manage to read scripture carefully and critically. Something can be inerrant (i.e., without error) without being literally true. Those who describe scripture as being inspired tend to distinguish truth (i.e., without error) from accuracy (i.e., literal truth), but then get all bollixed up in the popular meaning of those words.

As you read scripture stories, be not afraid to ask: "Does this text reveal God's will for humankind?" "Is this text literally true?" "Does my faith in God depend on this text being literally true?"

It's also important to know what the author of any particular text believes about the acceptable meaning and use of scripture. This is true for authors in antiquity as well as those currently writing about scripture and religion. The problem is we don't always know what those writing scripture were thinking or what they hoped their work would accomplish. Opinions are not facts, interpretations are not facts, and the fact of the matter is that we have precious little factual material about much that's recorded in scripture, but we do have some information thanks to manuscripts that have been unearthed. For example, most scholars have come to believe that the Red Sea mentioned in Exodus was really a marshy body of water more accurately called the Sea of Reeds.

Biblical scholars and theologians tend to agree that biblical writers wrote to record, revise, or interpret history; to inspire faith and righteousness; to persuade. How you understand their efforts will depend on what you choose to focus on whenever you read scripture.

If, as you read scripture, you focus on the impact of ancient civilizations and their languages, then you're within the domain of historical-critical analysis. If you're more interested in the impact of cultural artifacts (e.g., values, beliefs, ideas) and social variables (e.g., sex, gender, race, ethnicity, economic and educational status), then you've entered the world of social scientific analysis. If you focus on how language, structure, and tone are used in scripture stories, poetry, aphorisms, and letters, then you're in alignment with scholars who use techniques of literary criticism to understand and explain what they're reading. Whether you take any one or a combination of all these approaches, whatever you're able to glean will also depend on whose translation of scripture you read.

Which Translation to Read

Between the third and first centuries B.C.E., the Torah was translated from Hebrew into Greek for a version known as the Septuagint (LXX). The traditional story is that seventy-two elders translated the same text without consulting one another and miraculously managed to come up with the exact same translation, thus proving God's supremacy. In reality, translations involve human agency.

During the course of any English translation, decisions need to be made, for example, about which word in English most accurately captures its original meaning in Latin, which had been translated from Greek, which had been translated from Hebrew or maybe Aramaic, although most modern translators deal directly with the Greek or Hebrew. While I was writing this book, Catholic bishops in the United States were discussing how to retranslate the current English version of the Latin Mass. Debates became rancorous (or maybe just feisty) because some proposed translations, while accurate, became so unwieldy they undermined the value of using English. The point? In that situation, I'm not sure. Here, the point is that your choice of translation will shape your comprehension and appreciation of the text. Which translation to read? Plan to read several.[7]

For Christian scripture, you'll find eight different translations included on each two-page spread of *The Catholic Comparative New Testament* (New York: Oxford University Press, 2005).[8] I often consult this reference, which includes formal equivalent (word-for-word) as well as dynamic equivalent (thought-for-thought) translations. Be forewarned that the type font is punishingly small and difficult to read. My favorite translation for study and prayer is the New International Version (NIV). Although it's a dynamic equivalent translation, I've found its translation of the Tanakh strikingly similar to the new Jewish Publication Society translation of the Masoretic (traditional Hebrew) text.

My favorite translation for reading Hebrew scripture is *Tanakh: The Holy Scriptures* (Philadelphia, Pa.: The Jewish Publication Society, 1985). Not only is it translated directly from Hebrew, but it's formatted without customary columns. Chapters and verses are enumerated according to convention, but the text is formatted as a continuous narrative, making it easier to read through. Truth to tell, reading Genesis in this format made all the crime, passion, sex, intrigue, betrayal, incest, murder, mayhem, gore, vengeance, and violence of that book readily apparent and inspired me to keep reading God's word.

About Scripture and Me

When it comes to reading the Bible, I tend to be an equal-opportunity exegete. I believe there's great value in knowing historical context plus socio-cultural milieu. And I believe it's important to be curious about who wrote scripture, those who have interpreted scripture over the centuries, those who shaped the early church, and those who defined what Christianity would become.[9]

I read scripture in a variety of ways, letting personal needs and circumstances dictate method. Getting all historical-critical, social scientific, and being able to use the term "hermeneutic" properly doesn't stop me from appreciating the numinous nature of scripture.

I didn't exactly read the bible as a kid, even though our family library included the Soncino *Chumash* (yet another word for Pentateuch) and I attended religious education classes taught by rabbinical students as well as our congregation's rabbi and cantor. During college, I took a course called "The Bible as Literature." Loved it. As literature. I was generally disinterested in all things religious until my late thirties.

At some point reading scripture became important, but not because I made a rational decision to do so. For a gloriously scary period of time, I'd be yanked from sleep to check the scripture references that came to me in dreams. I still have the index cards on which I copied these verses. Yes, they still freak me out, but now not so much. As a result of those Holy Spirit encounters, I developed the habit of scribbling the dates and circumstances in the margins of the bible I use for prayer. I scribble different notes in the margins of bibles I use to write books and articles.

Ever the researcher, I shopped denominations before choosing a preferred provider of my Christian faith. As a result, I spent a few years cavorting with evangelical charismatic Christians who excelled at page-flipping scripture citation. While I had a somewhat visceral dislike for their tendency toward inerrancy and proof-texting, I sure learned how to access scripture quickly.

These days, I experience scripture as inspired and inspiring. I'm pleased that the venerable prayer practice of contemplative reading, *lectio divina*, is being actively revived among Catholics, and adopted by Lutherans and Episcopalians.

———◦∞◦———

FOR REFLECTION AND DISCUSSION

- How have your encounters with scripture changed over the years? How do you account for these changes?

- How does reading Hebrew scripture enhance your appreciation of Christian scripture?

- Which book(s) do you find most inspiring? Which passages do you return to again and again?

―――⋙〈ͻͻ〉⋘―――

TRY THIS

Developed during the second century and traditionally prac-ticed by monks, *lectio divina* offers a way of prayerfully engag-ing with the Word of God with the guidance of the Holy Spirit. Absolutely not an intellectual exercise, it's a wonderful spiri-tual practice to adopt. *Lectio divina* will get you out of your head and into your heart via Spirit. Here are the practical steps:

1. *Lectio* (read): in reverential silence, select a passage or word from scripture or, more accurately, allow the Holy Spirit to guide you to a selection.

2. *Meditatio* (meditate): silently ponder the meaning(s) of the passage or word you've selected, allowing it to resonate at multiple levels of awareness—as text, as poetry, as something you can't even define with mere words.

3. *Oratorio* (pray): allow meditation to transform into a prayer emanating from your heart rather than your intellect.

4. *Contemplatio* (contemplate): rest peacefully in the word and Word that has been revealed during the previous stages of *lectio divina*.

CHAPTER TWO

History Matters

Happy is the nation whose God is the Lord,
the people whom he has chosen as his heritage.

The Lord looks down from heaven;
he sees all humankind.

PSALM 33:12–13

You've probably heard the phrases "People of the Book" or "People of the Word" used to describe Jews and Christians because of our shared religious roots and fondness for narrative. Me? I tend to think of our Jewish forebears as "People of the Back Story."

The Israelites, or Jews, a people with twelve identified tribes at the start, had already logged more than two thousand years of vibrant existence before Jesus of Nazareth was born. And so, it should come as no surprise that Jewish history is filled with losses, triumphs, dislocations, and homecomings. From their very beginning, the people who would eventually become known as Jews sustained a unique relationship with God through direct revelation to patriarchs, matriarchs, kings, a long line of prophets, and ordinary people—like shepherds and carpenters. That so many Christians in the liturgical churches haven't been taught this essential back story is our great loss as followers of Jesus.

History matters and Jewish history matters a lot when it comes to understanding when, how, and why Christianity emerged as increasingly distinct from its Jewish origins during the first century. By about 75 C.E., the family of God had feuded itself into a religion that would be known as (Rabbinical) Judaism and a religion that, for at least a few centuries, would be known as Catholic Christianity. Two events significantly changed the religious landscape during the first century. How you understand these events will be shaped by your view of history.

Which History?

Viewing both secular and religious history through the lens of Christianity blurs Jewish history in some instances and makes it disappear completely in others. In addition to reading scripture critically, you'll need to cultivate an ability to view history through the lens of Judaism. What becomes visible once you're able to do this may surprise you.

Here's an exercise to help you develop this frame of reference: log onto your computer and type the key words "Jewish, history, timeline" into your web browser. Notice what pops up. You'll find timelines created by university or institute-based scholars, as well as ones compiled by individuals without academic training. You'll find timelines cobbled together by individuals and organizations with an obvious—or not so obvious—political agenda. It's important to recognize bias even if you can't specifically identify what it is!

While there's a high degree of uniformity about what periods of Jewish history are called (e.g., Pre-Exilic, Babylonian Exile, Rabbinical Era), the same cannot be said for how events

within these time periods are dated. Expect to find wide variations in dates for events before 2500 B.C.E. because no one
knows for an undisputed fact what really happened and
when. Our collective knowledge of this time period is limited
and quite literally fragmented—on bits and pieces of stone,
papyrus, and parchment.

How far back into Jewish history any timeline reaches
depends on the perspective of whoever has constructed the
chronology. Timelines beginning with the birth of Adam and
moving forward to include people or events for which there's
little or no archeological evidence are constructed from a
biblical-religious perspective. Timelines starting circa 2500
B.C.E. and providing the few dates that can be corroborated by
archeological research are constructed from a *biblical-historical*
perspective. Whatever ends up on a religiously oriented timeline depends on the religiosity of the compiler. Chronologies
compiled by ultra-Orthodox Jews do not read like those compiled by Jews in the Reform movement. (Judaism doesn't have
denominations; it has movements.)

As you scan timelines of Jewish history, please notice how
many names and events you have difficulty recognizing.
While Gamaliel's name might seem vaguely familiar from
Bible study because he trained Saul of Tarsus (Acts 5:34; 22:3),
how about the names of teachers like Hillel, Shammai, and
Akiva? During religious education classes, Jewish children rou-
tinely learn about great teachers and heroes who exist below
the Christian history radar. You may recollect Bible stories
about King Solomon's temple (1 Chronicles 28–29; 2 Chronicles 3–7), but you may be surprised to discover a long history
of temple construction and destruction, of exile and return. All
of it shaped Jewish religious and cultural identity, becoming
part of collective memory both conscious and unconscious,
then and now.

Dating Ourselves

You can contribute toward building goodwill and fostering Jewish-Christian dialogue by using notations that honor our shared history rather than ones asserting the primacy and centrality of Jesus the Christ. The abbreviations B.C.E. and C.E. are proper and preferred, especially when writing about interfaith issues. Consider using them in other contexts as well.

B.C.E. Before the Common Era

C.E. Common Era

B.C. Before Christ

A.D. In the Year of the Lord (*Anno Domini*)

Some Jewish history timelines include Christian people and events during the Common Era, but *only* if they've had an impact on Jews and Judaism. And, as you'll discover by reading Jewish history moving forward from the second century, much of Christianity's impact on Jews and Judaism is nothing for Christians to brag about. Scanning the woeful history of the Jewish Diaspora and the annihilation of the Jewish people reveals that the crucifixions and stoning of early Christian martyrs were hardly unusual, albeit awful, events. If they contemplate him at all, most Jews tend to view Jesus as yet another Jew, probably a prophet, murdered by authorities for causing trouble.

To get a better a sense of how deeply estranged the children of God's family have become, scan through a few timelines that purport to combine Jewish and Christian history. Again, whichever people and events are included will be defined by whoever constructs the chronology. Even the way events are characterized depends on who writes the history.

Historical Sensitivities

A rigorous education in Jewish history includes learning about discrimination and persecution usually, but not exclusively, by Christians. Beginning in the second century and continuing today in too many places, this long history of oppression includes being:

- forced to wear stars or other forms of religious identification;

- restricted to certain areas for living (i.e., ghettos);

- expelled from homes, settlements, and entire countries;

- excluded from certain professions, occupations, and social benefits;

- blamed for the crucifixion of Jesus;

- accused of slaughtering Christian boys during Passover and using their blood to bake matzoh; and

- told that the birth, life, death, and resurrection of Jesus proves that God has established a new covenant and Jews are no longer God's people— chosen or otherwise.

Entries about the Bar Kokhba rebellion (132–135 C.E.) provide a good example of what I mean.

An entry about this significant event in Jewish history from "A time-line of Christianity and Judaism" reads: "Jews, led by Bar-Cochba [sic], whom some identify as the Messiah, revolt against Rome."[10] Now here's the entry from a timeline provided by a Jewish online library: "Bar Kokhba rebellion (Second Jewish Revolt). Roman forces kill an estimated half a million Jews and destroy 985 villages and 50 fortresses."[11]

Here's another example—a description from *Timeline Charts of the Western Church*: "Second Jewish War (Bar Kochba Revolts). Jews protest, among other things, Emperor Hadrian's decision to make Jerusalem into the Roman city *Aelia Capitolina*."[12]

Many more examples reveal how even when Jewish and Christian history intersect, they're parallel universes of knowledge and reality. This is especially problematic when these historical realities remain separate for anyone who writes, teaches, and preaches about Christianity. Recent changes in the way Christians ought to properly understand their Jewish heritage and how those changes might, in turn, influence which selections from Christian scripture should be read during worship are due mostly to scholars engaged in Christian-Jewish dialogue efforts[13] (see Appendix C: Selected Documents on Christian-Jewish Dialogue).

History matters and it matters whose history you study. And yet, despite sectarian squabbles and all-out wars, Jews and Christians shared a common God, faith, and religious practice for nearly a century after Jesus died and became recognized by some Jews and Gentiles as the Christ. We continue to share more similarities than differences, although neither Christians nor Jews typically view it this way. Why not? The answer lies in knowing more about the Jewish world that Jesus was born into as well as the impact of two events after he became viewed as the Christ: 1) the Council of Jerusalem in about 48 C.E., and 2) the destruction of the Second Temple of Jerusalem by the Romans in 70 C.E.

Judaisms

While the ancient Israelites formed a monotheistic religion, it was never monolithic.[14] It would, in fact, be more accurate to say there were multiple Judaisms[15] during the first century.

Four major philosophical schools of Jewish thought shaped social power and authority when Jesus began preaching the Kingdom of God on earth. Two of them, the Pharisees and Sadducees, are mentioned frequently in the gospels. Both are mentioned in Luke's gospel and Acts of the Apostles; representatives from both formed the Sanhedrin (religious council).

You're probably most familiar with the Pharisees because they appear frequently throughout Christian scripture. Their beliefs about life, death, ethical behavior, and religious practice were shaped by the teachings of Hillel (ca. 60 B.C.E—20 C.E.). The Pharisees were Torah scholars and teachers. The Sadducees were priests and aristocrats in charge of Temple worship and influenced by Shammai (ca. 50 B.C.E.—30 C.E.), a teacher known for his harshness and rigidity. It's easy to confuse these sects (or what some scholars would prefer to call "schools") or think they're interchangeable because they're often mentioned in tandem within Christian scripture, although John's gospel tends to lump them together as "the Jews."

In reality, Pharisees were religious moderates. They were committed to ongoing, lively debate about how the Law of Moses ought to be interpreted, recognizing there could be circumstances for going beyond the letter and into the heart of the law. This is something to keep in mind while reading gospel stories about Jesus' encounters with the Pharisees. For example, stories like ones about the permissibility of healing on the Sabbath (Luke 13:10–16; Luke 14:1–6) are usually preached in churches to illustrate the antagonism of the Pharisees toward Jesus. As someone raised Jewish, I tend to view these stories as examples of the Pharisees doing unto Jesus as they were doing unto one another—debating Torah.

As "high priests" (Acts 4:1; 5:17), the Sadducees were religious fundamentalists whose strict adherence to Temple rituals will make more sense after reading about the priesthood in Leviticus (21–22) and Numbers (3:5–10; 4:4–20; 8; 18). They rejected the authority Pharisees granted equally to written scripture and oral tradition. Sadducees, who accepted only the Five Books of Moses as scripture, were literalists who insisted, for example, that the Shema[16] be recited while reclining because it was written in Deuteronomy that the prayer should be said "when you lie down and when you rise" (Deuteronomy 6:7b).[17] (Since Sadducees were legalists, it's not historically accurate to fling the epithet "Pharisee" at a doggedly legalistic Christian. In fact, calling someone a "Sadducee" might raise the level of discourse above the usual mud-slinging!)

Pharisees stressed love for God, God's mercy, prayers of the heart, and emphasized the essential importance of the commandment to "love your neighbor as yourself" (Leviticus 19:18). Pharisees also believed in the eternal relationship between God and God's creation; the resurrection of the body after death, and the existence of angels. Sadducees rejected these teachings.

The Pharisees' and Sadducees' conflicting beliefs about the resurrection of the dead became the pivotal issue the apostle Paul would draw upon when he stood before the Sanhedrin (Acts 22:30-23:6–10). "Brothers, I am a Pharisee, a son of Pharisees," he declared. "I am on trial concerning the hope of the resurrection of the dead" (Acts 23:6). This entire story is, in fact, a great illustration of how vehemently these two sects opposed one another. The dispute around this difference of belief became so violent that Paul had to be removed for his own safety (Acts 23:6–10).

What you probably never learned at Sunday school or from any formal catechism[18] is that the historical person of Jesus was more in alignment with the Pharisees because of the content and style of his teaching. This might seem odd until you know what Pharisees believed and taught, and then reread Christian scripture with this in mind. Notice, too, how Jesus shares meals with Pharisees (Luke 14:1). A group of fellow Pharisees warn him about Herod's murderous intentions (Luke 13:31). So what if he calls both the Sadducees and the Pharisees a "brood" or "generation of vipers" (Matthew 3:7)? He calls his own disciples people of "little faith" (Luke 12:28).

The Pharisees weren't the only Jewish group in and around Jerusalem during the first century. Jesus of Nazareth would've appealed to members of the Zealot sect. They were revolutionaries—zealously antagonistic to the Romans to the point of near-total self-extinction through warfare with the Romans. Some biblical scholars also note Jesus' compatibility with the Essenes. This group connected the promise of resurrection to the coming of God's kingdom during end times and emphasized the need for repentance. They were, however, monastic and isolated in their desert community, so it's difficult to know how much contact they may have had with Jesus.

Here's the most important point: Jesus of Nazareth lived and taught within a thick matrix of Judaisms[19] that would become even more complex after his crucifixion, death, and resurrection redefined him as the Christ.

The Way

Once resurrected from the dead, Jesus became Christ for his Jewish followers. The wondrous shock of seeing Jesus alive compelled Mary of Magdala and the other apostles to form a new sect known as The Way (Acts 9:2; 19:23) or Yeshua-followers.[20] Gentiles also became attracted to The Way and, after his own revelation, Paul began actively seeking out Gentiles for conversion. But many of these Gentiles were pagans who brought along beliefs, rituals, and traditions that would have to be integrated into this new form of Judaism. Gentiles did not observe central aspects of Mosaic Law and this, among other things like pagan pantheism, generated tensions among the apostles as they went out to fulfill the Great Commission (Matthew 28:16–20). The gathering where the status of Gentiles was debated and resolved, the Council of Jerusalem, would be a defining moment in Jewish history.

Council of Jerusalem

Peter was committed to spreading the good news of Jesus as Christ, but wondered about the wisdom of reaching out to Gentiles. They were pagans unschooled in the Law of Moses; they did not observe the dietary laws or participate in purification rituals. They'd freely eat food that had been placed before—and therefore polluted by—idols. Their men were uncircumcised; their sexual practices wild. Truly the *ruach hakodesh* was doing extraordinary things, but what was Peter to make of it all? During prayer time on an empty stomach (which maybe had something to do with it), Peter received a vision about eating impure or unclean animals and birds. After calling out to God in protest, Peter heard a voice say, "Do not call anything impure that God has made clean" (Acts 10:15, NIV).

Did this mean, then, that he *should* meet with Cornelius, a Gentile who had become a God-fearing, righteous man (Acts 10:22–33)? Did this mean that God would purify a Gentile's heart by faith alone? You can read about Peter's struggle to reconcile his religious observance with his emerging identity as leader in Acts of the Apostles (10, 11). These chapters will help you understand the significance of what happened during the Council at Jerusalem (Acts 15), because although Christianity wasn't a separate religion until the end of the first century, the Council's actions served, in effect, to move the new Jewish sect in that direction.

The cutting-edge issue was circumcision. Paul, Barnabas and, because of his encounter with Cornelius, even Peter argued with Pharisaic representatives to exempt Gentiles from that particular "yoke" of Jewish Law (Acts 15:10). Instead, they argued for the enforcement of other signs, customs, and laws. "We should not," declared James, who presided over the Council, "trouble those Gentiles who are turning to God, but we should write to them to abstain only from things polluted by idols and from fornication and from whatever has been strangled and from blood" (Acts 15:19–20). The Council's letter made it possible for Gentile men to follow Jesus without being circumcised as a sign of God's covenant with Abraham (Genesis 17:1–14). Other rituals, primarily baptism, were established to affirm Christian affiliation and identity. I wonder what would've happened if the vote had gone the other way. Just a wild guess, but maybe if the Council had ruled Gentiles must be circumcised, we'd all still be Jews?

Disputes between Peter and Paul about how Gentiles could and should become part of The Way continued after the Council adjourned. Peter focused his ministry on brother and sister Jews (Galatians 2:8). Paul, who received his revelation about Jesus as Christ after the resurrection and a career of harassing and suppressing Jewish followers of Jesus, focused his ministry on Gentile believers (Galatians 2:8).

Although Peter had been in alignment with Paul, Barnabas, and James about exempting Gentile believers from circumcision, he was more conflicted about abandoning dietary laws. Yes, Peter had shared meals with Gentiles. He had been less than observant when it came to dietary laws, but they were tightly woven into his identity as a righteous man. Although Peter's dissonant behavior is sometimes viewed as evidence for his repudiation of *halakhah* (Jewish law), I view it the ancient equivalent of eating bacon while away from one's kosher home!

For Jews then and now, righteousness was not separate from Torah law. As a follower of Jesus who would have been in alignment with the Pharisees, Peter was open to debate and moderation. Still, when it came to determining the extent to which Gentiles needed to follow Jewish customs and laws, he opposed Paul. Paul's account of this pivotal dispute appears in his letter to the community of Galatia. More about his break with fellow Pharisees can be found in his letters to the Corinthians and Philippians.

In Galatians, Paul wrote that while faith in Christ Jesus did not change the fundamental covenant between God and Abraham, "now that faith has come, we are no longer under the supervision of the law" (Galatians 3:25 NIV). For Paul, neither circumcision nor dietary laws had any meaning; what mattered now was carrying one another's burdens and living by the Spirit (Galatians 5). No one, he argued, "will be justified by the works of the law" (Galatians 2:16).

Writing to the Corinthians, Paul challenged the *meaning* of dietary laws. "'Food will not bring us closer to God.' We are no worse off if we do not eat, and no better off if we do. But take care that this liberty of yours does not somehow become a stumbling-block to the weak" (1 Corinthians 8:8–9). In Philippians, he dismissed circumcision and other laws as useless trash. *Tzedakah* (righteousness), he declared, does not come from the law but through faith in Christ (Philippians 3:5–11).

To what extent did these differences damage the relationship Peter and Paul had with one another? Scholars believe Peter was crucified in about 64 C.E. and Paul was beheaded in about 67 C.E. Some scholars point to passages in letters to the Corinthians and Galatians to argue that their rifts were healed (e.g., 1 Corinthians 3:21–25; Galatians 2:14–6:18). In any event, Jews who didn't follow Jesus continued drifting from those Jews and Gentiles who did. Family ties were ruptured completely when the Second Temple was destroyed in 70 C.E.

The Second Temple Is Destroyed

With the destruction of the Second Temple of Jerusalem, everything changed for all Jews, including those following Jesus. Not their enduring belief in one God—that had already survived millennia of multiple disasters. Previous temples had been built, destroyed, and rebuilt. But this catastrophic event forever changed the location, structure, and character of Jewish worship. This time, destruction was total in unprecedented ways.

The Shoah

In a history filled with catastrophic events, the Nazi annihilation of Europe's Jewish population stands out. In addition to physically wiping out millions, the Shoah radically exposed the deep persistence of anti-Semitism (hatred of Jews as an ethnic-racial group) and anti-Judaism (hatred of the Jewish religion) resulting from centuries of unchallenged Christian triumphalism. The Shoah forced Christians and Jews to ask more and different questions about God, human suffering, forgiveness, and the importance of collective memory; this process continues now, especially as survivors die of old age. The Shoah compelled all Jews to consider what it means to live and practice post-Shoah Judaism.

Shoah, also Sho'ah or Shoa (Hebrew for "destruction"), is the preferred term for what has been called the Holocaust. The original word for holocaust, the Greek *holokauston*, refers to "a burnt sacrifice offered to God" and generally appears in scripture whenever Torah-mandated sacrifices are mentioned. Shoah is used to militate against the theologically offensive implication that the Nazi "Final Solution" had anything to do with pleasing God.

By obliterating the Temple, the Romans obliterated every-thing that went along with it—the role of the priesthood for *kohanim* (priests) and *levites* (associate priests); all worship organized around the ritual slaughter of animals; the physical locus of religious identity. There would be no Temple reconstruction and return to Temple worship as there had been after the destruction of the First Temple in 586 B.C.E. What emerged from the wreckage was a different type of Judaism that could not include the followers of Jesus for a number of reasons.

While synagogues had existed as gathering places for study and debate during the Temple period, these houses were now the only location for Jewish study, worship, and prayer.

As Jewish followers of Jesus began developing rituals (e.g., the Lord's Supper), they became increasingly likely to gather with Gentile followers in the early *ecclesia* (congregations) that scholars call "house churches." Within five years of the Temple's destruction, house synagogues began expelling Jewish followers of Jesus who insisted he was the Christ, forming their own separate community. *Rabbis* (teachers) replaced priests as the religious and spiritual leaders of the Jewish people.

Paul intensified the emergence of a separate religion, not only in the content of his letters but in their structure. His epistles open with greetings "to the church of God." His audience is addressed as "saints." The traditional priestly benediction, "The Lord bless you and keep you" (Numbers 6:24–26) is replaced by closings such as "The grace of our Lord Jesus Christ be with your spirit" and "Peace to all of you who are in Christ," and "May the grace of the Lord Jesus Christ, and the love of God, and the fellowship of the Holy Spirit be with you all." While this served to build church, it also served to move early Christians further away from their Jewish roots, as did Paul's referring to Jews as "dogs . . . evil workers . . . those who mutilate the flesh" (Philippians 3:2). Those who argued for the preservation of at least some Jewish law, custom, and tradition were denigrated the "Judaizers."

The Judaizers

Those who insisted Gentile followers of Jesus had to follow the Torah and be circumcised like all other Jews were known as "Judaizers." After all, they reasoned, Jesus was a Jew and therefore those who followed him needed to live like Jews. Despite the outcome of the Council of Jerusalem, this issue did not go away. The Judaizers accused Paul of repudiating Mosaic Law and being, in essence, a traitor to the faith of his forebears.

Although many Jewish rituals were sustained within early Christian worship, during the second century Polycarp, the bishop of Smyrna, warned against Judaizing (i.e., imitating the Jews). Disputes began emerging about whether the Jewish calendar should be used to calculate the date of Easter. The Council of Nicea (325 C.E.) further severed connections between Judaism and Christianity by officially changing the date of Easter from that of Passover. Christians would became progressively more ignorant about their Jewish heritage until Christian-Jewish dialogue emerged toward the end of the twentieth century (see Appendix C: Selected Documents on Christian-Jewish Dialogue).

What do you see when you read this history through the lens of Judaism? What I see and recognize are the familiar signs of a family feud spinning out of control. In all of it I observe the demonizing that emerges when disagreements turn into deeper disappointments and are then viewed as betrayals. I see the seeds of Christian anti-Judaism and Jewish self-preservation, sown in the Council of Jerusalem, taking root in the charred remains of the Second Temple. That so much of Jewish belief and tradition has survived and can be seen at all in Christian practices is a miracle—with a bit of mystery thrown in. I'll focus on this more specifically in the next chapter about worship practices.

We Are Where?

Whenever I mention the Early Church, I'm basically referring to whatever form of Christianity was being practiced by Jews and Gentiles for approximately a hundred years after Jesus of Nazareth was crucified. This period of time includes the:

- Apostolic Age and all events that distinguished and separated Judaism from Christianity during those years (c. 35–65 C.E.)

- apocalyptic destruction of the Second Temple of Jerusalem (70 C.E.)

- beginning of Christians' expulsion from Jewish houses of worship (75 C.E.)

- evolution of Christian communities into churches with leadership and governance (ca. 92 C.E.)

- establishment of Christian rites (ca. 101 C.E.)

(See also Appendix A: Timeline: Christianity Emerges from Judaism).

FOR REFLECTION AND DISCUSSION

- When did you first discover that Jesus was Jewish? How did that discovery come about?

- How does your understanding of the gospels change once you know Jesus studied and taught in the tradition of Rabbi Hillel?

- What do you imagine might have been different had key aspects of Jewish law and practice prevailed at the Council of Jerusalem and subsequent church councils?

TRY THIS

Notice what happens to Christian scripture when the Hebrew names of essential people are restored and Mary becomes Miryam, Jesus becomes Yeshua, and Peter becomes Kefa. Make this come alive by translating from Greek to Hebrew all the names used in just a few chapters from Luke and Acts of the Apostles. To experience what happens when the entire text is de-Hellenized, take a look at: David H. Stern (translator), *Jewish New Testament: A Translation of the New Testament that Expresses its Jewishness* (Clarksville, Md.: Jewish New Testament Publications, Inc., 1989).

CHAPTER THREE

Worship

Ascribe to the Lord the glory of his name;
worship the Lord in holy splendor.

PSALM 29:2

For the ancient Israelites, praise and thanksgiving to the almighty God who delivered them from Egyptian bondage took place under the sun, moon, and stars. They welcomed safe passage through the Sea of Reeds, manna from heaven, and water from boulders with songs of praise and dances of ecstatic gratitude. They celebrated miracles with tambourines, shofars, and drums. That's what worship looked and sounded like.

Worship became more formal after Moses hiked up Mount Sinai to meet God face-to-face. Moses returned to base camp with detailed instructions for holy living (Leviticus 11–25); guidelines for atoning for sin and giving thanks with burnt offerings of cattle and grain (Leviticus 1–7); specifications for worship space and everything in it; details for crafting priestly garments; and how-to's for setting everything up (Exodus 35:4–40:33). No need to cart around graven images. God was everywhere.

Everything was designed to make worship portable while the Israelites wandered toward the land promised to them. The tabernacle with its richly hued, jeweled fabrics; the Ark[21] carrying the Decalogue inscribed on stone; the lamp stand; a table for pitchers and bowls; washing basins; the altar for burnt sacrifices; Aaron's rod and priestly garments—all portable, although it's hard to imagine schlepping a stone altar (Exodus 20:25). And according to scripture, there was a lot of schlepping. When the Israelites broke camp and crossed the Jordan river on their travels, the priests carried the Ark of the Covenant (Joshua 3:11–17).

Trumpets no doubt come to mind whenever you hear or read the words "battle of Jericho." Those seven trumpets were followed by the Ark of the Covenant (Joshua 6:1–20). Later, when they were up against the Philistines, the Israelites retrieved the Ark from Shiloh to protect them—not a smart strategy since they were slaughtered and the Ark was captured by the Philistines (1 Samuel 4:1–11). In the first book of Samuel, you can read about why the Philistines returned the Ark (1 Samuel 5–6). Tales of transport and Ark mojo continue throughout the second book of Samuel. Check it out.

An established worship space with permanent sacrificial altars, a sacred inner sanctuary, grand hallways, staircases, and courtyards wouldn't be built until the Israelites arrived in Jerusalem, and then not until the fourth year of King Solomon's reign during the tenth century B.C.E. (1 Kings 6). The Law continued to structure and guide daily life but community worship became temple-based. No longer would the Tent of Meeting or its contents have to be carried from place to place (1 Chronicles 23:25–26). For a while, anyway.

When the First Temple (a.k.a., the Temple of Solomon) was destroyed by the armies King Nebuchadnezzar in 587 B.C.E., everything of value within it was stolen and transported to Babylonia along with anyone surviving the devastation (2 Chronicles 36: 2–21). After returning to Jerusalem from Babylonian Exile in 537, the Israelites slowly but surely built another great temple and dedicated it in 515 B.C.E. (Ezra 3–6; Nehemiah 2–8). This was the Second Temple later renovated by King Herod the Great nearly twenty years before Jesus was born and is the temple featured in gospel stories.

Sacrificial offerings may have ended forever when the Second Temple was destroyed in 70 C.E. but worship continued. Synagogues had already been established during the Babylonian Exile for Torah reading, *bet midrash* (study), and *bet tefilah* (prayer), so they also became *bet knesset* (assembly). All these activities took place in houses of worship that were, quite literally, houses, that is, private homes—there was no distinction between home and synagogue. Prayers replaced live sacrifices and burnt offerings, although the timing and structure of daily worship remained the same. Eventually, synagogues became separate buildings decorated with ritual objects replicating those transported throughout the millennia. Today, the structure of worship space and liturgy as well as the language of prayer remains remarkably unchanged among traditional, observant Jews.

For at least five years after Jesus died, his Jewish and Gentile followers studied and prayed together at house synagogues with the rest of the Jewish people. Once expelled from these synagogues because of their belief in Jesus as Lord and Savior, they gathered as a separate community in homes, often those of wealthy women, to prayerfully share the ceremonial meal of bread and wine using the familiar structure of *berakot* (blessings/benedictions). The word *ecclesia* originally referred to church as the people, not a building. Centuries passed before Christian churches were built and formal liturgies established. Once they were, guess what those churches and liturgies seemed like?

Church as *Bet Midrash*

Here's what I tote to church when I'm traveling light: my very own Missalette-devotional combo, a purple pen, a yellow highlighter, and my prayer notebook. If I'm sticking around for devotions, I'll bring a bible.

I've been known to dog-ear pages of my Missalette-devotional combo as the Word is being proclaimed. I'll jot down debate points during the homily, even though I know I won't leap up out of the pew to argue. Instead, I circle verses in purple or highlight them in yellow. I ponder how, if given the opportunity, I might crack open the Word for fellow congregants. I wonder if I'm in the presence of blog fodder. I'll later write about my wonderings on my blog.

I am not being inattentive or disrespectful. I'm honoring my longstanding devotion of learning and commentary. Whenever there's a break in *tefilah* (prayer), I default to *midrash* (interpretation).

Worship Space

Nearly everything you see in your church and much of what you experience during liturgy (i.e., order of service) is not only rooted in Judaism, but can still be observed and experienced in a variety of ways at traditional synagogues. Obviously not the crucifix or cross, but really and truly just about everything else. Once you look at your church sanctuary through the lens of Judaism, you cannot help but see it in a new way, one more ancient than you probably imagined. I hope you'll come to see what I do whenever I attend *any* liturgical church—worship space that's more similar to than different from what I experienced growing up in the Reform movement of Judaism. Here's the biblical and first-century provenance of what's in your church sanctuary.

Tabernacle

Christ is the Word made flesh and his presence is with us in the consecrated bread and wine stored in the tabernacle. The tabernacle will be either on a high altar against the eastern wall of the sanctuary or off to the side on its own altar or pedestal. Something is horribly wrong if you fail to notice the tabernacle when entering your church's sanctuary or separate chapel. It should capture your attention, open your heart, and lift your spirit.

Your church's tabernacle may be shaped like a miniature church or dome. It may have golden doves etched on its door or attached to its sides. It may be inlaid with precious or semi-precious jewels. If so, the origin of this embellishment as well as any veils, covers, or curtains for protection is easily traced back to God's instructions for building the Ark of the Covenant (Exodus 25:10–22) and the tabernacle to shield it (Exodus 26:1–37). At that point in Jewish history, the tent-tabernacle served to protect the *aron hakodesh* (holy chest) that held the stone tablets inscribed with the Ten Commandments. It also protected the *omer* (a dry measurement approximately one gallon) of manna kept before the Lord in perpetuity to remind the Israelites how God had kept them fed (Exodus 16:32–34).

To this day, the Ark that holds the revealed Word of God on parchment scrolls is the central focal point in every synagogue sanctuary. Visit a synagogue or look at images online and you'll see a large cabinet against the eastern wall. This is the Ark. In some synagogues, it's covered by a richly embroidered *parochet* (curtain). (In gospel accounts, this is the Temple curtain that split in two either right before or immediately after Jesus died [Luke 23:44–45; Matthew 27:50-52; Mark

15:37–38].) In others, its doors are ornately carved or otherwise embellished. Each *sefer Torah* (handwritten scroll) is dressed in its own velvet or brocade cover. Think vestments, which disappeared from Judaism when the priesthood ended and spiritual leadership became more broadly available to members of the community. The silver shield hanging over its draped front recalls the breastplates worn by priests during Temple times (Exodus 28:15–30).

The Sacristy

Yes, it's a small room. Yes, it's usually located behind the altar. Yes, it's where vestments, sacred vessels, altar linens, incense, the processional cross, unconsecrated bread and wine, and lectionaries are stored. Yes, it usually includes a special sink. Yes, it seems as if only clergy may enter. (And yes, it may seem as if they spend too much time in there.) Nevertheless, the sacristy is not the modern-day version of the *Kadosh Hakadashim* (Holy of Holies). Really. Not. Anyone may wander in there. God's *casa es su casa*.

Sanctuary Light or Presence Lamp

Roman Catholic, Lutheran, and Anglican/Episcopal churches keep a lamp burning perpetually by the tabernacle where consecrated bread or "reserved sacrament" is stored. These lamps are either suspended from the ceiling by a chain, bolted to a wall, or set on a lamp stand. They're typically red, although there's no canonical reason for that color.

No matter what your church says the sanctuary lamp represents (e.g., the light of Christ, eternal presence of God), it originated in God's ordinance that a lamp be kept "burning before the Lord from evening till morning . . . among the Israelites for the generations to come" (Exodus 27:21, NIV; see also, Leviticus 24:1–4). In synagogues, the *ner tamid* (eternal light) hangs centered above the Ark. It, too, is red.

Altar-Table

The altar-table in your church might be a moveable free-standing wooden table or a fixed free-standing marble platform. If you attend a very old church or your home church is a cathedral, the altar may be covered by an ornate *ciborium* or *baldachino* (canopy structure).

These days, you can get a good sense of a church's theological stance by noticing the placement of the altar-table and whether it's fenced in and relatively unapproachable because of chancel railings surrounding it. The altar-table has become more open, accessible, and simple in nearly all liturgical churches built during the late twentieth century. Here's something to ponder: the original instructions for building the (portable) sanctuary table called for lots of gold overlay and moldings (Exodus 25:23–29). We think worship took place around an open, accessible, and simple table in house synagogues and churches.

You won't find an altar in a synagogue because it was eliminated along with sacrificial offerings. The *bimah* (reading platform) might, however, resemble an altar-table if it has been built wide enough to unroll the Torah scrolls further than they would at a lectern. In traditional synagogues, the bimah is covered by a *mappah* (table covering) to keep the Torah from lying directly and irreverently on plain wood. Think church altar linens and liturgical actions to protect the consecrated communion.

Worship services are sometimes led from the bimah or another podium called an *amud*, which would correspond to the church's pulpit or ambo. Traditional synagogue sanctuaries also have a smaller table that looks like the small side table found in the sanctuaries of Christian churches and used to hold everything that will be used during celebration of Holy Communion. They appear, generally in Conservative and Orthodox synagogues, to fulfill God's ordinance, "Put the bread of the Presence on this table to be before me at all times" (Exodus 25:30, NIV; see also, Leviticus 24:5–9). These tables also hold wine and water for ceremonial washing; more about ablutions in Chapter 4 (Baptism).

Candelabrum

God's declaration, "Let there be light" (Genesis 1:3) is reflected in the multitudinous candle stands you'll find in liturgical churches, probably (but not exclusively) next to the tabernacle. Go ahead and tally up how many branches are on the *menorah* (candelabrum) in your church's sanctuary. If it has six or seven, your church is honoring instructions for crafting this lamp stand from Exodus (25:31–40) and Numbers (8:1–4).

Ask a liturgist why there's a menorah on the altar and notice the answer you receive. You may be told the seven-branched candlestick represents the "perfect life of Jesus" or the seven gifts of the Holy Spirit.[22] Then again, the size and configuration of lamp stands might be determined by your church's budget. Still, isn't it nice to have a scripturally based rationale?

In synagogues this candelabrum is somewhere in the sanctuary space near the Ark or by the bimah. If it has nine branches, it's a *chanukia*. Some say the chanukia symbolizes the burning bush; others say it represents the miracle of oil lasting for eight days during the Maccabees' rebellion; the ninth candle, the *shamos*, is used to light the others. In either event, everyone seems to agree the chanukia has more branches to preserve the sanctity of the Temple menorah.

Decorative Symbols

You can trace the origin of *reredos*, or church decorations, above or behind the altar to Hebrew scripture verses about decorating the Arks with cherubs of hammered gold (Exodus 25:18–22). Hebrew scripture is filled with descriptions of sumptuous furnishings and other décor as well as monumental architecture (1 Kings 7).

In churches, the type and number of decorative furnishings will vary between and within denominations but it's not unusual to find stained glass windows, icons, tapestries, and statues that may include images of a descending dove, flames, lilies, roses, the Star of David, and monograms (e.g., IHS, ✸) on them. Whether your sanctuary has a cross or a crucifix, and whether the crucifix depicts Christ as suffering servant or the risen Christ also varies and reveals your church's theological stance. Roman Catholic churches recognize both images by having one type of crucifix stationary and the other carried in the liturgical procession.

Statuary was and is conspicuously absent from Jewish worship space because of the first commandment, "You shall not make for yourself a sculptured image, or any likeness of what is in the heavens above, or on the earth below, or in the waters under the earth" (Exodus 20:4, JPS). This prohibition did not extend to decorative or representational art, although neither humans nor animals were represented, possibly because idols took those forms. The Golden Calf incident certainly didn't advance the cause of sculptors (Exodus 32). Artistic craftsmanship was viewed as a gift of the Holy Spirit (Exodus 35:30–31). Anyone able to create with precious metals, gemstones, wood, and yarn had clout during ancient times (Exodus 35:30–35).

In contemporary synagogues you'll find artistic representations of the Ten Commandments and other Jewish artifacts (e.g., Torah scrolls, a menorah) as well as letters of the Hebrew alphabet. The twenty-first letter of the Hebrew alphabet, "shin" (𝒲 or 𝒲) is a popular choice because of its relationship to *Shaddai*, God's name revealed to Abraham, Isaac, and Jacob (Exodus 6:2–3).

Which Ten Commandments?

Rarely am I at a loss for words but I was struck momentarily dumb when during a workshop for catechists I was asked, "Do Jewish people believe in the Ten Commandments?" I quickly described the Sinai Event and its significance for Jews. I didn't have time to get into the fact that images of the Ten Commandments take various forms.

In synagogues you'll find images with either five or all ten commandments on each tablet. Although Jesus echoed Hillel when streamlining the commandments to two, the Decalogue informs moral theology for Christians. In Roman Catholic, Lutheran, and Anglican/Episcopal churches, the first three commandments are usually depicted on one tablet and the rest on the adjacent tablet. But this is not set in stone (or acrylic resin). You'll find differences in the representations.

Is there an image of the Ten Commandments in your church sanctuary? If so, what does it look like? Where is it?

Liturgical Calendar

The church's worship year is organized around a set calendar and it should come as no surprise that Roman Catholics, Lutherans, and Anglican/Episcopalians use the same liturgical calendar and the same three-year cycle of readings. These churches begin the Temporal Cycle and church year with

Advent. The rest of the calendar is divided into seasons commemorating the birth, life, death, and resurrection of Jesus the Christ.[23] Sunday, declared the new Sabbath by Constantine in 321 C.E., is the key marker for determining the timing and duration of Advent, Christmas, Winter Ordinary Time, Lent, Easter, Pentecost, and Ordinary Time. Our Jewish heritage is readily apparent in vigil observances, which are rooted in the Jewish tradition of beginning each holy day at sundown the previous evening. And of course the seven-day week is an enduring legacy of Judaism.

Liturgical church calendars also include a Sanctoral Cycle memorializing extraordinary women and men who lived and died in the service of Christ.

Here's where you'll find differences among the liturgical churches. For example, Lutherans and Anglican/Episcopalians commemorate Martin Luther on February 18; Roman Catholics do not for reasons that should be obvious. Anglican/Episcopalians commemorate William Wilberforce on July 30; Lutherans and Roman Catholics do not. Everyone puts the apostles, including Mary Magdalene, on their Sanctoral calendar. The calendar of the Lutheran Church-Missouri Synod (LCMS) features more Jewish patriarchs and prophets than anyone else, which is even more amazing if you know about Luther's unrepentant anti-Judaism.

The only possible glimmer of Judaism's influence relative to the Sanctoral Cycle may have to do with the fact that these memorials are observed on the person's *Yahrzeit* (Yiddish: anniversary of a death). While there's no shortage of Jewish martyrs, the concept of sainthood doesn't exist in Judaism—no matter how many vaguely anti-Semitic jokes you've heard about Jewish mothers.

The Jewish calendar, based on the sun and the moon, shaped the life of Jesus and his followers. The appointed feasts of the Lord they observed required pilgrimage to the Temple in Jerusalem and involved one or more days of prayer, sacrifice, fasting, and feasting (Leviticus 23:1–44). Gentiles and pagans within the Roman orbit followed the solar calendar mandated by Julius Caesar, a custom lasting until Pope Gregory XIII constructed his own updated version during the sixteenth century. The Gregorian calendar became the dominant way to organize the year when church and state were indistinguishable, and remained so after church and state separated. As a result, the Jewish calendar remains generally unknown to most Christians, although its impact as a lunar calendar is apparent in the rule for determining the proper date of Easter using the first Sunday after the first full moon after the solar equinox.

Appointed Feasts of the Lord
According to the Torah

Festivals and other events, all of which involved burnt offerings, were synchronized with significant seasons in the lives of farmers and shepherds. Since three of the major God-appointed feasts on the Jewish calendar are tied to harvests, it's neither fair nor entirely accurate to pick on pagans every time foliage or fire shows up during Christian holy days.

	Jewish Observance	*Christian Observance*
Sabbath	Sundown Friday	Sundown Saturday
Passover and Feast of Unleavened Bread	15–22 Nisan	Holy Week
Feast of Weeks/Spring harvest (Shavuot)	6–7 Sivan	Pentecost

Feast of Trumpets *(Rosh Hashanah)*	1–2 Tishri	1st Day of Advent
Day of Atonement *(Yom Kippur)*	10 Tishri	
Feast of Tabernacles/ *Fall Harvest (Succoth)*	15–21 Tishri	

Liturgy

No matter what it's officially called, Roman Catholics, Lutherans, and Anglican/Episcopalians share an order of service and formula for prayer. Liturgical churches use signs and symbols (a.k.a., sacramentals) to create and sustain reverence for all that's holy. We share ways of reinforcing community (a.k.a., the Body of Christ) while nurturing the individual's relationship with God. Again, many of these practices can be traced back to Temple Judaism. Christians and Jews may have some central theological differences—although not as many as we commonly think—but when it comes to practicing and expressing faith, we're more similar than different. Here's how the practices of our Jewish forebears have shaped Christian liturgy.

Order of Worship

Many Christians have fought and some have even died over differences about the proper focus and meaning of Christian worship. Theologians have built entire careers arguing the fine points, but this tempestuous history should not obscure today's practical reality: the order of worship is fundamentally the same for the Mass celebrated by the Roman Catholics and Eastern churches, the Service of Holy Communion celebrated by Lutherans, and the Holy Eucharist celebrated by Anglican/ Episcopalians.[24]

As it was for our Jewish forebears, Christian worship is by definition a community event. It involves rites, special prayers, and ritual actions that find their origins in Jewish worship before the birth of Jesus:

- *Introductory Rite*
  - Gathering
  - Greeting

- *Penitential Rite*
  - Confession
  - Prayer for Forgiveness

- *Liturgy/Ministry of the Word*
  - First Lesson/Reading from Hebrew Scripture
  - Psalm (Sung)
  - Second Lesson/Reading from Christian Scripture
  - Third Lesson/Gospel Reading
  - Sermon/Homily
  - Creed
  - Prayers of Intercession/Prayer of the Faithful

- *Liturgy/Ministry of the Sacrament/Eucharist*
  - Exchange of Peace (location is currently being decided for Roman Catholics by the Vatican)
  - Preparation of the Table
  - Offertory/Collection/Offering of the Gifts
  - The Great Thanksgiving/Eucharistic Prayer
  - Lord's Prayer
  - Eucharistic Prayer/Breaking of the Bread
  - Communion

- *Dismissal Rite*
  - Post-Communion Prayer
  - Dismissal

At first glance you might think this worship service structure doesn't have much to do with Judaism except for a reading from Hebrew scripture and psalms. After all, the Creed and the Lord's Prayer are essentially Christian and although Judaism has a time-honored tradition of blessings over bread and wine, the word "communion" is freighted with Christian meaning (see Chapter 5). But Christian liturgy emerged out of a structure composed for synagogue worship by Ezra the Scribe and his court during the fifth century B.C.E.

I Love a Parade

During the Second Temple period, Jewish worship was conducted by priests who could trace their lineage to Aaron (Exodus 40:12–33; Leviticus 8–9). Torah assigns detailed priestly duties to the tribe of Levi and its clans (Numbers 3:1–37).

The Levitical priesthood ended in 70 C.E. and worship was primarily led by rabbis. Although early Christian communities were fairly democratic, hierarchical distinctions soon began emerging. By the second century, the term "priest" was back in use by Christians. By the early third century, the hierarchy of bishop, presbyter, and deacon was firmly established; minor orders including lectors, acolytes, and doorkeepers had become widespread.

Who walks down the center aisle at the beginning of your church's worship service? Depending on the formality of your liturgy, the procession will include acolytes (carrying a processional cross, incense, candles), lay eucharistic ministers, lector, cantor, priest/minister and associate priests/assisting ministers, deacons. Some are ordained, others are laity. Their liturgical functions

> can be traced back to the thirteenth century B.C.E., as can every piece of ceremonial clothing they wear (Exodus 39:1–31).
>
> If you turn to face and follow this procession, you're echoing the tradition of facing and following the Torah scrolls as they're paraded around the sanctuary before being read. Fortunately—or not—the custom of kissing the scrolls has not been extended to celebrants et al.

Prayers and Benedictions

Before and during Temple times, sacrifices were accompanied by prayers and blessings mandated by Torah law. These prayers and blessings would have been woven into the fabric of daily life for Jesus and his followers at times corresponding to morning, afternoon, and evening sacrifices. They would have recited the Decalogue and the *Shema* (Deuteronomy 6:4–9). They would have prayed the *Amidah* (standing), an omnibus prayer also known as the *Shemoneh Esrai* (Eighteen Blessings). During morning services, they would have prayed *Tachanun* (penitential prayers).

Jewish worship included songs of adoration and praise—*kodosh! kodosh! kodosh!* (holy, holy, holy);[25] a psalm of the day and more psalms for special festivals; more benedictions including ones before and after reading from the Torah, and *haftorah*, which are readings from *Nevi'im* (The Prophets). Worship concluded with this priestly blessing: "The Lord bless you and protect you! The Lord make his face to shine upon you and be gracious unto you! The Lord lift up his countenance toward you and grant you peace!" (Numbers 6:24–26, JPS). There's more, all of which continues during traditional synagogue worship today.

Any of it seem very familiar to church-going you? It should! It's very much like our order of liturgy. The daily schedule of prayers, blessings, and readings also lives on in the Liturgy of the Hours, an essential prayer practice of vowed religious communities and clergy that some laity also follow. These days, you can have each day's Liturgy of the Hours sent directly to your computer, phone, or other electronic device. I often "attend" morning prayer, vespers, and compline via Twitter!

Did Jesus Pray in Hebrew?

Hebrew was and is the sacred language of Judaism, firmly established as such in its current written form by Ezra the Scribe during the fifth century B.C.E. Given the Hellenistic (Greek) influence on the Jews during that time, Jesus was probably also conversant in *Koine* Greek. He was certainly able to speak and teach in Aramaic, the everyday language spoken in Palestine at that time. Did Jesus speak Latin? There's no evidence of that, but the Gospel of John, written circa 90 C.E., notes that the sign Pilate had nailed to the cross along with Jesus was written in Aramaic, Latin, and Greek (John 19:19–20, NIV).

Expressing Reverence

What's the proper balance between exuberance and quiet reverence during worship? When should we shout for joy, sit in silence, or fling ourselves prostrate before the altar? Should our eyes be opened or closed during prayer? Our hands lifted or pressed together? What should the presider be doing with his or her hands? Should we bow or bend down onto one knee and if so, which one? Should we stand or kneel when communion is being consecrated? Who gets to make the sign of the cross over anything? Who may kiss the Lectionary after reading? Who may and should wear a head covering? These are just some ways we express reverence during worship. Although many are mentioned in Hebrew scripture, they've mostly emerged as a matter of custom in Christian churches. None are mandatory, although they may have been at points in church history and might feel that way now at your church. You will not go to hell for failing to make the sign of the cross or wearing a head veil in a Roman Catholic Church, nor will you be eternally damned for crossing yourself during a Lutheran liturgy. You might, however, get some strange looks from congregants for wearing a *kippah* (beanie-like cap), especially if it's scarlet and a bishop is presiding.

Although people have always knelt during prayer, especially prayers of supplication, standing attentively was the preferred posture for Temple and synagogue worship. Pagans knelt down before idols. Regardless of which movement's services you visit, you'll find a lot of standing, sitting, and swaying during Jewish worship. Conservative and Orthodox Jews reverence the Torah during its procession through the congregation by touching the cover with a *siddur* (prayer book), their *tallit* (prayer shawl), or their hand and then kiss whatever has touched the Torah.

Color Me Sacred

Color Symbolism in Hebrew Scripture

Green: Natural growth and life; rest; freshness

Purple: Royalty

Red/Scarlet: Cleansing or purification, but also sin; blood; war; plague; vengeance

White: Purity and refinement; righteousness

Color Symbolism in Christian Worship

Green: Hope for eternal life

Purple/Violet: Penance and purification

Red/Scarlet: Suffering and martyrdom but also divine love and royalty; fire; blood; Holy Spirit

Rose/Pink: Joy

White: Purity; innocence; glory; joy and triumph

FOR REFLECTION AND DISCUSSION

- How does your understanding of the liturgical calendar change once you know Jesus and his early followers lived in synch with the Jewish calendar?

- How might your worship experience shift if all prayers, blessings, and readings were proclaimed in a foreign language?

- What might a Jewish visitor to your church find familiar? Which, if any, worship practices do you imagine a Jewish visitor might find off-putting or downright offensive?

---ᴑ/ᴑ/ᴑ---

TRY THIS

Try cultivating the spiritual habit of saying prayers and blessings or benedictions throughout your day from the moment you wake up, before every activity, and before you go to sleep at night.

You can easily find prayers and blessings from the Christian tradition in books or online. You might want to try praying the Liturgy of the Hours for a month . . . a week? Or, you might want to discover and add some of the traditional Jewish *berakhot* (benedictions/blessings) to your prayer repertoire. There are plenty from which to choose! You could also use transliterations to pray them in Hebrew and notice the spiritual impact of doing so.

CHAPTER FOUR

Baptism

Create in me a clean heart, O God,
and put a new and right spirit within me.

Do not cast me away from your presence,
and do not take your holy spirit from me.

PSALM 51:10–11

Being a desert people, the Israelites were acutely aware of water in all its forms—rivers, rain, floods, seas. They had to pay attention; the presence or absence of water had a profound impact on daily life. Stories featuring water as a source of life and death flow throughout Hebrew scripture. Epic chronicles of redemption feature water.

The Bible narrative of creation begins with the Spirit of God hovering over the waters (Genesis 1:2), waters teeming with living creatures (Genesis 1:20–21), waters rising up from the earth to stimulate life—all before God gets around to creating humankind (Genesis 2:6). Flood waters destroy all life except what Noah has gathered onto the ark at God's behest (Genesis 7). The sign of the first and everlasting covenant between God and all of creation was the glistening result of water—a rainbow (Genesis 9:12–17).[26]

Water ebbs and flows through the book of Exodus. Baby Moses is fished out of the Nile (Exodus 1:22–2:10). Water turns to blood (Exodus 4:8–9); transports a plague of frogs from the Nile into Egyptian homes (Exodus 8:1–15); hardens into hail to destroy the people, livestock, and harvest of Egypt (Exodus 9:13–23). After being miraculously parted for the escaping Israelites, the Sea of Reeds becomes a watery grave for Pharaoh's army (14:21–31). Flood waters of the Jordan River ebb so the Israelites may continue traveling to Canaan (Joshua 3–4). Water is featured in stories about God's mercy at Marah and Meribah, despite human doubt and disobedience (Exodus 15:22–26; Numbers 20:5–11). God only knows what stories of water sought and found were never recorded.

Water was as meaningful in emerging ritual as it was in daily life. Toward the end of Exodus you'll find references to full body immersion for the consecration of the *kohanim* (priests) and washing rituals for entering the Tent of Meeting and approaching the altar (Exodus 29:4; 30:17–21).

For kohanim and laity alike, God's injunction, "Be holy, because I am holy" (Leviticus 11:44, 45) was tied to a core emphasis on cleanliness at multiple levels of meaning. If you've ever wondered about the origins of the expression "cleanliness is next to godliness," you'll find answers in Leviticus where rituals for maintaining physical and ceremonial cleanliness are spelled out.

To the modern reader it might seem as if these are simply rules for managing personal hygiene, body emissions (e.g., Leviticus 14:1–9; 15:1–32), and good housekeeping (e.g., 14:33–53). We, after all, are blessed with knowledge about germs. Our forebears didn't make these distinctions. Most biblically based laws about physical cleanliness were tied to notions of spiritual purity (e.g., worthiness or readiness for worship) with the presumption that anything physically unclean could put everything at risk for defilement.

You'll find *mitzvot* (commandments) about washing and bathing repeated throughout Numbers, along with detailed descriptions of immersion, pouring, and sprinkling rites for purification from sin (e.g., Numbers 19). In the Tent of Meeting, the wash basins were portable; rivers and other natural sources of water (e.g., "living water") were used for the *mikvah* (ritual bath). When Solomon's Temple was built, wash basins and full immersion pools became permanent fixtures with water flowing into them from natural sources. The courtyard positioned by the Water Gate held a "molten sea" with two thousand baths large and deep enough to completely cover the body (1 Kings 7:23–26).

The destruction of that Temple in 586 B.C.E. did not end these rites. If anything, immersion, pouring, and sprinkling rites became especially important during the Babylonian Exile. Oral tradition credits Ezra the Scribe with decreeing that all men fully immerse themselves in a mikvah before synagogue prayer or study, a practice that continued after the Temple was revived. Ezekiel prophesied about the power of water to cleanse the Jews of all impurities, including those resulting from contact with or actually succumbing to the worship of idols (Ezekiel 36:25).

Not only did water-based rituals saturate Jewish life by the first century C.E., but most sects practiced full body immersion prior to worship. The Essenes, who may have been one and the same as the Dead Sea sect at Qumran, were particularly concerned about maintaining a high degree of purity and may have immersed themselves daily. Whether those two sects were synonymous, and whether John the Immerser belonged to either, remains the subject of scholarly debate.[27] In any case, John, who practiced full immersion in the Jordan

River, preached the need for this water baptism for the repentence of sins (Luke 3:2–9).

While John wasn't the only prophet performing such purification rituals, he was the only one to baptize Jesus. Scripture reveals his jitters about having the manifest destiny of doing so. John was humbled by the prospect, alerting his followers, "I baptize you with water; but one who is more powerful than I is coming; I am not worthy to untie the thong of his sandals. He will baptize you with the Holy Spirit and fire" (Luke 3:16).

When Jesus arrived at the Jordan River, John hesitated. Why was he baptizing Jesus and not the other way around? To fulfill all righteousness, Jesus explained (Matthew 3:13–15). In other words, to ensure Jesus' right relationship with God, which is how righteousness is defined in Judaism. Christians would come to believe that Jesus himself was the personification of righteousness, becoming so during immersion. After all, as Jesus rose from the waters of the Jordan, the ruach hakodesh descended on him in the form of a dove, and a voice from heaven proclaimed, "You are my Son, the Beloved; with you I am well pleased" (Luke 3:22).

After his crucifixion and resurrection, Jesus instructed his disciples to make disciples of all nations by purifying them through water immersion "in the name of the Father and of the Son and of the Holy Spirit" (Matthew 28:18–20). If he had been speaking in Greek, Jesus would have used *baptize*, the common word for "wash by immersion." During the Feast of Shavuot alone, Peter called thousands to repentance *in the name of Jesus the Christ*, promising them the gift of the Holy Spirit, and baptizing them (Acts 2:38–41). But the mikvah for purification in these holy names wasn't immediately considered an initiation rite. Another and more ancient form of initiation already existed for (male) followers of Jesus: circumcision.

Clean or Unclean?

By the time Jesus was born, commandments about cleanliness and purity had been in effect for at least 1,200 years. Then, as now, some probably pondered the deeper meaning of these laws. Then, as now, some automatically went through the motions of ritual observance. Then, as now, folks within each group looked askance at one another. Enter, Jesus.

Jesus challenged how people thought about ritual practices, inviting them to consider what they were doing and why. When is holiness present? What might cause it to become absent? He used logic and metaphor to make and remake his points. He explained, for example, that eating without observing hand washing rituals or eating unclean food did not automatically make anyone impure. The stomach was not connected to the heart; the stomach did not generate "evil intentions" (Mark 7:14–23). Hand washing out of reverence or because of actual yeech? Yes. Hand washing as empty ritual? No.

Circumcision as Covenant

In Genesis, God makes two of the great covenants (i.e., promises). Considering the topic of this chapter, isn't it interesting that God made the first great and abiding promise after a flood? Never again would all life and all the earth be obliterated by water (Genesis 9:11–17). Next promise?

God will remain forever as the one and only God of everyone descended from Abraham and Sarah (Genesis 17:1–8).

Male circumcision would signify this covenant (Genesis 17:9–14) established for all time when Abraham, his son Ishmael, and every man in Abraham's household were circumcised (Genesis 17:23–27).

Moving forward, the *brit milah* (covenant of circumcision) would be performed on baby boys eight days after their birth (Genesis 17:12–14; Leviticus 12:3). As for Sarah, "I will bless her, and moreover I will give you a son by her. I will bless her, and she shall give rise to nations; kings of peoples shall come from her." (This news makes Abraham fall on the ground laughing [Genesis 17:15–17] which, had the technology existed, he might have conveyed to Sarah by texting, "ROTGL.") Thus circumcision became an abiding covenant, followed forever except when it wasn't and God had to issue a reminder (e.g., Joshua 5:2–9).

Although circumcision was already practiced in many parts of the ancient world, it became the distinctive symbol for all Jews, uniting them with one another and with God. As a result, anti-Jewish groups throughout history have tried abolishing this rite of initiation into Jewish identity. The Romans, for example, prohibited the practice after destroying the Second Temple. During the fifth century, King Sisbut of Spain ordered Jews baptized instead of circumcised. Typically, their other option was death. And so forth and so on through the ages.

Today, circumcision has become a widely accepted practice among non-Jews, but this hasn't diminished its significance as a sign of God's covenant with the Jewish people. Contemporary Jews who are otherwise non-observant continue to fulfill this commandment at a home-based ceremony commonly referred to as a *bris*. (In case you're wondering, let me be the one to tell you there's absolutely no connection between the words "bris" and "brisket.")

Did Jesus Have a Bris?

Was Jesus circumcised? Of course! We believe that God took the form of a man to have the whole human experience. The human form of that man was Jewish. Jesus was circumcised on the eighth day in accord with Mosaic law. We celebrate his bris as a holy day, despite St. Paul's insistence that the physical practice was an irrelevant sign of faith and belief in Jesus as the Christ (see Chapter 2). And whether they realize it or not, the secular world also celebrates Jesus' circumcision—on New Year's Day.

For centuries, the Feast of the Circumcision of Our Lord commemorated both the circumcision and naming of Jesus. Since the mid-twentieth century, this Holy Day of Obligation for Roman Catholics has been called the Feast of Mary, Mother of God. Lutheran and Eastern Rite churches have, however, retained the traditional name of this festival because of its indisputable mention in scripture (Luke 2:21–24). Orthodox churches customarily pray for infants eight days after birth in a ceremony called "Prayer for the Signing of a Child Who is Receiving a Name on the Eighth Day After His Birth." Among Anglicans the event is celebrated as the Festival of the Holy Name or the Naming and Circumcision of Jesus.

Now take another look at the liturgical calendar from December 25 through February 2. Roman Catholics, Lutherans, and Anglican/Episcopalians celebrate the entire cycle of Jewish ritual observance during this time. A boy is born (December 25), then circumcised and named (January 1). The Jewish observance is completed by the Presentation of the Lord, originally known as the Feast of the Purification of Mary or Candlemas (February 2), an event in alignment with post-birth purification laws set forth in Hebrew scripture (Leviticus 12).

Naming Names

This well-known passage about Jesus' holy name appears in Paul's letter to the Philippians: "Therefore God also highly exalted him and gave him the name that is above every name" (Philippians 2:9).[28]

Although I could write an entire book on this point alone and I'm sure someone already has, let me note that throughout scripture names are changed to signify transformation. Possibly the best example in Hebrew scripture is when God renames Abram, Abraham and Sarai, Sarah (Genesis 17:5, 15).

In the Jewish tradition, boys have always had their names conferred during the *brit milah*; girls at birth. Although Jewish identity is conveyed matrilineally (i.e., through the mother), Hebrew names for girls and boys reference the father (e.g., Miriam bat Amram; Isaac ben Abraham), although the mother's name is used for a *misheberach* (prayer for healing).

According to Christian scripture, the angel who told Mary about her awesome fecundity got to name the newborn Jesus (Luke 1:31–33). Baby Jesus was named during his circumcision in accord with Mosaic law (Luke 2:21–24). Does any of this have anything to do with the Roman Catholic and Orthodox tradition of conferring special baptismal names? Who knows for sure? That custom was established during the sixteenth century by the Council of Trent.

Baptism as a Sacrament

Christians agree about the central importance of baptism for establishing Christian identity. Baptism is the rite of entry into the *catholic* (universal) Christian community, one that establishes that in Christ we are one body. The Great Commission could not be more clear: "Go therefore and make disciples of all nations, baptizing them in the name of the Father and of the Son and of the Holy Spirit" (Matthew 28:19). Nevertheless, this did not prevent differences from emerging over the centuries, nor has it prevented pesky persistent dissension between liturgical and non-liturgical churches.[29]

During the first century, Torah-mandated purification rites shaped how followers of Jesus were initiated into The Way. Purification (i.e., making something clean and holy) was seen as an essential element of initiation (i.e., making something new). This initiation-purification rite involved water in specific, well-established ways that were either adopted or adapted over time. By the third century, the sacrament we call "baptism" was considered a uniquely Christian rite of initiation. Over the centuries and, to some extent continuing today, discussions and disagreements among the followers of Jesus swirl around:

- *When should baptism take place?* Adulthood? Infancy? Adolescence? Infant baptism didn't become an issue until children were born to adult followers of Jesus the Christ. Could someone be re-baptized?

- *What sort of preparation is required?* Fasting? Vigil? Formal repentance?

- *Where should baptism take place?* Natural waters were a given, but did the development of house churches mean building baptisteries? Would they be pools like the mikvah? Fonts or basins?

- *How should baptism be performed?* Full immersion was a given for quite a while, but should baptism include the laying on of hands? Anointing with oil? In what sequence? Should the practice of being fully immersed while naked be continued? Should special garments be worn to enhance the meaning of "putting on Christ"? Since baptism signified entrance into Christian community, could and should groups be baptized? Did the community need to be present as a corporate witness?

- *Would there be an accompanying rite?* Other than baptizing in the name of the Father, and of the Son, and of the Holy Spirit, what form should it take? Which prayers, blessings, and oaths should be included?

- *Who could perform baptism?* The first apostles, certainly, but after that? Could any baptized disciple baptize new disciples? Was this properly the role of elders? Priests and deacons? Women?

- *What did baptism confer?* An entirely new person was born in the waters of baptism, but was the Holy Spirit conveyed as well?

These disagreements became more nuanced as Christianity developed into a separate religion with its own but not necessarily a totally distinctive structure of leadership and liturgy. Times of persecution, schism, and reformation necessitated changes in the location, ways, and means of baptism.

Baptism was considered one of seven sacraments during the twelfth century. Four centuries later, Luther and Zwingli argued baptism was one of two sacraments, the other being the Eucharist, which prompted the Roman Catholic Church to re-declare it one of seven sacraments during the Council of Trent, which convened periodically between 1545 and 1563 C.E. By the seventeenth century, the Church of England was in alignment with the reformed churches of Europe—baptism was one of two sacraments. It took three more centuries for Roman Catholics, Lutherans, and Anglican/Episcopalians to become more rather than less in alignment about baptism.

Currently, the baptism rite for Roman Catholics, Lutherans, and Anglicans/Episcopalians is similar in structure and content. We agree that spiritual formation and participating in Christian community is a lifelong process. We may not yet share full communion, but we do have a greater degree of mutual recognition, although mutual recognition can wobble at times. One recent example is the 2008 statement issued by the Vatican's Congregation for the Doctrine of the Faith invalidating baptisms administered in anything but "in the name of the Father, and of the Son and of the Holy Spirit." The Roman Catholic Church does not recognize baptisms administered "in the name of the Creator, and of the Redeemer and of the Sanctifier" or any other formula using gender-neutral language. On the other hand, the Roman Catholic Church recognizes as valid the baptismal rites of all mainline Christian faiths and does not require "re-baptism" from those who enter the church from other communions. We are baptized as Christians, not members of a particular denomination.

Mikvah and Contemporary Judaism

Although Temple-based requirements for ritual purity ended when the Second Temple was destroyed, the practice of ritual immersion continued. During the second century, ritual immersion became part of a rite for anyone, male or female, converting to Judaism, although proselytism wasn't and isn't practiced by Jews. In addition, the mikvah played an important function in the domain of marital sexuality. It still does.

Torah law prohibits sexual relations between spouses while the wife is menstruating. Currently this practice includes a period of abstinence for seven days after her bleeding stops. Full water immersion on the eighth day restores her to ritual purity. (An unmarried woman is only required to go to a mikvah before her wedding.) Note: she is not taking a bath, she's transforming her spiritual status. In fact the ritual involves becoming impeccably clean before entering the mikvah waters. These laws are followed by observant Jewish women and the accompanying prayer is: "*Blessed are you, O Lord our God, King of the Universe, who has sanctified us by His commandments and commanded us to perform the ritual immersion.*"

The content of debates about observing laws of "family purity" during the nineteenth century shifted during the twentieth century as Jewish women challenged the accuracy of focusing on purity instead of cycles of fertility. Do the arithmetic and you'll see that Jewish laws about sexual abstinence optimize the probability of procreation during intercourse.

Here's another interesting factoid: having a working mikvah is so important that if the community can afford to build either only a synagogue or a mikvah, under Jewish law, the mikvah is constructed first.

More Water-based Rituals

Judaism's legacy is also visible in several ablutions (ceremonial washings) practiced by liturgical churches today. Some are regular features of liturgy (e.g., lavabo) and others make an appearance at special times during the liturgical year (e.g., foot washing, sprinkling).

Hand Washing

Hand washing rituals have their source in Hebrew scripture as do details about washing basins (Exodus 30:17–18) and their use. Aaron and his sons were the first recruited into priestly service requiring real and symbolic cleanliness: "When they go into the tent of meeting, or when they come near the altar to minister, to make an offering by fire to the Lord, they shall wash with water, so that they may not die. They shall wash their hands and their feet, so that they may not die: it shall be a perpetual ordinance for them, for him and for his descendants throughout their generations" (Exodus 30:20–21).

Even before the Temple's destruction, hand washing rituals were part of daily life for Jews (e.g., upon waking, before meals, before eating bread, after meals, before formal prayers). During festivals like Passover, hand washing rituals were accompanied by special prayers. These rituals were sustained with one important difference as Christian liturgy emerged. Instead of being everyone's ritual responsibility during the fellowship of believers that included the breaking of bread and prayer, *lavabo* (from Latin: "I will wash") became performed exclusively by priests.

In your church, a water pitcher, washing basin, and a lovely little laundered fingertip towel will be on the credence table next to the altar. Extra points for historical accuracy if your church uses a bronze lavabo dish! The lavabo ceremony involves an acolyte/altar server pouring water over the celebrant's fingertips as the celebrant prays the final verses of Psalm 26. Sometimes this prayer is audible, perhaps too often it is not. Sometimes the priest simply prays, "Lord, wash away my iniquity, cleanse me from my sin."

Observant Jews continue this mitzvah today as originally prescribed, praying: *"Blessed are you, O Lord our God, King of the*

Universe, who has sanctified us by His commandments and commanded us concerning the washing of the hands." If a descendant of the kohanim reads from the Torah during synagogue services, Jewish orthopraxy requires both water pouring and hand washing in preparation.[30] According to tradition, a human, not a faucet, must pour the water to recall the ancient practices. Get this: water is poured three times over first the right hand and then the left one.

Foot Washing

Foot washing was an essential feature of hospitality during biblical times (see: Genesis 18:1–5). It also became a God-given requirement for priestly preparation before worship (Exodus 30:19–21) and remained so as long as the Temple existed. And although liturgical churches reenact the Last Supper's foot washing event on Holy Thursday, this ceremony is not the exact equivalent of the Torah-mandated practice for priests. The Holy Thursday ritual, which did not become common until the fifth century, is tied to John's gospel account of Jesus washing and drying his disciples' feet (John 13:1–17), a story that does not appear in any other gospel.

Here we find Jesus attempting, once again, to teach his disciples something about the deeper meaning of cleanliness. He's also trying, once again, to teach them about fellowship, mutual regard, and equality. Jesus is no quitter! Look, he says, I'm the teacher but see how I'm washing your feet? You ought to be doing that for one another because "servants are not greater than their master, nor are messengers greater than the one who sent them" (John 13:16).

Contemporary Jews do not observe foot washing rituals.

Sprinkling Practices

The *asperges* (sprinkling rite) that became customary during the ninth century was initially a rite to purify places and things, as well as people. Today, "high" church liturgy may include sprinkling the altar, clergy, and congregants before the Eucharist is consecrated. Many Roman Catholic, Lutheran, and Anglican/Episcopal churches customarily sprinkle the assembly with water each Sunday during Easter. In liturgical churches, funeral services are begun by sprinkling water over the coffin.

Getting sprinkled with holy water during liturgy is supposed to remind you of baptism. The rite generally takes place after the Renewal of Baptismal Vows during the Easter season or on holy days when baptism is featured (e.g., January 11, The Baptism of Our Lord). Hopefully, feeling drops of water landing on you will indeed reawaken lovely memories of your baptism. Or perhaps not so lovely if you were a volatile little screamer.

Although the term "asperges" (Latin: thou shalt sprinkle) comes from the Latin version of Psalm 51:7, many more references to sprinkling practices involving hyssop appear in Hebrew scripture. Detailed descriptions in Leviticus and Numbers provide examples of purifying things as well as people (e.g., Leviticus 14: 1–9; Numbers 19:1–22). Sprinkling rituals are not part of Jewish worship today. To be entirely accurate, asperges isn't practiced today with biblical rigor by churches. Doing so would involve slaughtering a ram, bull, lamb, goat, or bird and then mixing its blood into the water first before flinging it around the sanctuary.

Holy Water

The Roman Catholic custom of having a small font filled with holy water at church sanctuary entrances and inside a home's front door is just that—a custom. These holy water fonts have symbolic meaning as a sacramental, something that resembles or points to a sacrament rather than an official sacrament of the church. Those who observe this tradition dip their fingers in the water and bless themselves (or others) with the sign of the cross. Think of it as a mini-immersion ritual, which harkens back to major immersion rituals sourced in Judaism.

It may seem like a stretch but the Jewish practice of hanging a mezuzah on each doorway is similar because it, too, invites all who enter and leave to be mindful of God's presence. Unlike a holy water font, a mezuzah fulfills the commandment to love the Lord with heart, soul, and strength (Deuteronomy 6:4–9). A box with Deuteronomy 6:4–9 and Deuteronomy 11:13–21 scribed onto kosher parchment is affixed to the doorway's right side. It's customary to kiss the tips of one's fingers before lightly touching God's word as a sign of reverence.

About My Baptism

By the grace of God and the spiritual wisdom of those shepherding me at the time, my baptism took place within two weeks of me finally saying, "Alrighty, Jesus! I believe you are who you say you are." No wimpy pouring or sprinkling rite for me! I was baptized by full immersion three times, each plunge in the name of the Father, and of the Son, and of the Holy Spirit. The sanctuary happened to be cold and the waters warm, so steam was generated whenever I was raised up out of the baptismal pool.

Well over a decade later I can easily conjure up the felt memory of awe as external mist displaced internal fog. Well over a decade later I can easily hear my friend Joan proclaiming, "I love the Lord, for he heard my voice; he heard my cry for mercy. Because he turned his ear to me, I will call on him as long as I live. The cords of death entangled me, the anguish of the grave came upon me; I was overcome by trouble and sorrow. Then I called on the name of the Lord: 'O Lord, save me!'" (Psalm 116:1–4, NIV). I can less easily remember stripping off soaking wet white clothing and blow drying my hair.

I was in my early forties, so I tell people I was old enough to know what I was doing and that's basically true. I knew being baptized meant entering fully into a new life of faith. Without ever having heard the words of the Roman Rite, I knew I was being claimed for Christ. Having decided to stop drowning, I welcomed the promised resuscitation. But while I may have been old enough to know what I was doing, I never anticipated how my life would change as a result of receiving the sacrament of baptism.

Baptism Timeline
(Common Era)

ca. 27   Jesus baptized in the Jordan River by John the Immerser (Baptizer).

1st c.   Some Jews and Hellenists become baptized and consider themselves followers of Christ Jesus.

3rd c.   Infant baptism first mentioned in *On Baptism* by Tertullian.

Baptismal preparation involves fasting and vigil.

Baptism ritual includes confessing sin, renouncing Satan.

Infant baptism becomes common.

First house-church baptistry.

Baptism distinguished from laying on of hands.

Re-baptism controversy.

Council of Carthage forbids women to baptize.

5th c. Baptism performed by priests as well as bishops.

12th c. Baptism considered one of the seven sacraments.

15th c. Baptism formally declared a sacrament (Council of Florence).

16th c. Baptism is one of only two sacraments (Luther and Zwingli).

Baptism removes stain of original sin (Council of Trent).

Baptism is one of seven sacraments (Council of Trent).

17th c. Baptism is one of only two sacraments (Church of England).

FOR REFLECTION AND DISCUSSION

- How does the time and way baptism is performed change the way you understand or appreciate baptism?

- How would your experience of baptism change if it were not a once-for-all-time event but something to be practiced regularly, like mikvah?

- Did Jesus have a last name? If so, what was it? Keep in mind that "Christ" is not Jesus' last name but a title (i.e., Messiah) and that he was called by his Hebrew name, Yeshua.

TRY THIS

While we profess how we "acknowledge one baptism for the forgiveness of sin" when we recite the Creed, consider treating every—or almost every—face washing or bath like a mini-baptism. We do, after all, renew our baptismal promises during Easter so why not intone, "I embrace my baptism in the name of the Father, and of the Son, and of the Holy Spirit" when you wash up? Alternatively, you could honor your Jewish heritage by praying, *"Blessed are you, O Lord our God, King of the Universe, who has sanctified us by His commandments and commanded us to wash."*

CHAPTER FIVE

Holy Communion

. . . the Lord is gracious and merciful.
He provides food for those who fear him;

he is ever mindful of his covenant.

PSALM 111:4–5

Take one early story about angelic visitation in the form of dusty, hungry strangers (Genesis 18:1–10). Include years of slavery followed by forty years of desert wandering while dependent on daily sustenance falling from the sky by God's mercy (Exodus 16). When you then add centuries of forced exile plus ghettoization to the historical mix, welcoming all to share sustenance and receive shelter becomes a moral imperative. As a matter of Torah law, the Israelites were commanded to practice hospitality, especially to strangers (Deuteronomy 24:17–22). Meals were opportunities to recognize physical and spiritual nourishment, "You shall eat your fill and bless the Lord your God for the good land that he has given you" (Deuteronomy 8:10). The after-meal grace was specifically intended to guard against the human possibility of forgetting God's sovereignty (Deuteronomy 8:11–18).

Hospitality was a deeply embedded feature of Jewish life by the time Jesus of Nazareth appeared on the scene. Although some specific wordings were finalized later, the obligation to say grace before and after meals, as well as food-specific blessings during meals, had been established.

But as we know from anthropologists, it's also true that rigid cultural rules about who could eat with whom, who was allowed to sit where, and who was permitted to preside over meals had emerged. Years of tribal dissension and political differences among religious sects added to tensions, making it impossible for certain Jews to break bread together, let alone with despised outsiders (e.g., pagans, tax collectors).

Jesus challenged the cultural rules that threatened to undermine the sacred nature of hospitality intended by Torah law (Luke 10: 38–42; 14:1–24). He fed thousands without regard for who was attending (Matthew 16:29–11; Luke 9:10–17). He healed during meals (Luke14:1–14), and ate with "sinners" (Luke 19:1–7). The author of the letter to the Hebrews included radical hospitality on his list of exhortations to the Jewish followers of The Way, "Do not forget to entertain strangers, for by so doing some people have entertained angels without knowing it" (Hebrews 13:2, NIV). Indeed, it's within this conceptual framework of hospitality that the Jewish roots of Holy Communion make the most sense.

Behold Your Meal

Scripture includes accounts of memorable meals. Some were fear-of-the-Lord (i.e., awesome) events, others foreshadowed revelations of God's sovereign power. Here are some Torah stories worth rereading through the lens of faith. Notice what happens after everyone burps their appreciation:

Genesis 18:1–10	Abraham and Sarah feed three visitors.
Genesis 25:19–34; 27:1–39	Jacob and Esau bargain over stew.
Exodus 12:1–30	Moses and Aaron convey God's festival instructions.
Numbers 11:4–35	The Israelites challenge the food menu.

Bread

Bread is a major feature of the Jewish people's story of redemption—the miraculous deliverance from Egyptian slavery. In Exodus, we read how the Israelites were instructed to prepare bread dough without yeast for quick, easy transport (Exodus 12:8, 39). Bread provided physical and spiritual nourishment as the adventure continued. During forty years of desert wandering, God rained down a daily portion of bread. The Israelites called it *manna,* and scripture describes it as tasting like wafers made with honey (Exodus 16:4; 31). To commemorate this God-given gift of sustenance, the Israelites were commanded to keep a portion of manna at the altar of the Lord in perpetuity (Exodus 16:32–34). Even though Moses reminded God's chosen people "that one does not live by bread alone, but by every word that comes from the mouth of the Lord" (Deuteronomy 8:3), bread had special sacred meaning.

During Temple times, twelve loaves of bread replaced the omer of manna in the sanctuary. Every day, priests placed the loaves on the altar, taking out a piece of *challah* (portion of the dough) to fulfill the commandment, "as the first yield of your baking, you shall set aside a loaf as your gift; you shall set it aside as a gift like the gift from the threshing floor. You shall make a gift to the Lord from the first yield of your baking, throughout the ages" (Numbers 15:20–21, JPS).

After the Second Temple was destroyed, the ritual of preparing and blessing bread shifted to the home. Separating out the challah portion was no longer a priestly ritual. Challah was still separated out, but the olive-sized piece was blessed and burned in the family hearth. This ceremony became something Jewish women fulfilled as part of their special duty to bake bread for the Sabbath, something you might want to ponder during a worship service you hear celebrants mention "the work of human hands."

Bread of Life—Mine!

Bread is a major food group in Jewish homes—at least it was when I was growing up. Whole wheat bread hadn't yet become a suburban staple in the 5700s (a.k.a., 1960s). We had the requisite loaf of white Wonder Bread, but it paled in comparison to everything else stuffed into the bread drawer.

I remember bakery-fresh loaves of German pumpernickel, Russian black bread, caraway seeded rye bread, marble rye bread, and challah; bagels and bialys; and *pletzel* (onion board). My Aunt Matty was a creative, prolific baker but whenever supper ended and Uncle Henry said, "I'm ready now for my cake," she served him two slices of rye.

Wine

Setting aside references to wine as cheering gods and mortals (Judges 9:13) and gladdening the heart (Psalm 104:15), the press on grapes in Hebrew scripture is not exactly positive.

You'll find strict prohibitions against kohanim drinking wine or any other fermented drink before entering the sanctuary (Leviticus 10:8–9). You can also find at least one story about the dire consequences of drunkenness (e.g., Genesis 9:18–25). By the time wise counsel for daily living was collected and recorded in Proverbs, it was generally understood that "Wine is a mocker, strong drink a brawler, and whoever is led astray by it is not wise" (Proverbs 20:1). Still, wine was part of worship, both somber and festive. It was a feature of celebratory meals and enhanced the spirit of hospitality. While wine had the potential to generate liveliness, it was never viewed as symbolically representative of blood. And what about blood?

Blood clearly represented life (Genesis 9:4–6) and when spilled on the altar, was proper atonement (Leviticus 17:11). On the other hand, Torah law clearly forbade the Israelites and aliens living among them from consuming any blood from any creature (Leviticus 17:12–14). And yet, at least two synoptic gospel writers report Jesus lifting the cup of hope at the end of the seder and saying, "This is my blood," without anyone tossing his or her wine cup against the wall in revulsion (Matthew 26:28; Mark 14:24). According to Luke's gospel, the disciples were more interested in figuring out who would betray Jesus (Luke 22:21–23) and arguing about who among them was the greatest (Luke 22:24).

Decades later, to make the case for Jesus as sacrificial lamb, the author of Hebrews explained that by his own blood, Christ obtained eternal redemption for all (Hebrews 9:11–28). Wine is never mentioned and is mentioned with customary caution in Paul's letters. Weighing in the controversy over clean and unclean food, Paul explained to the church in Rome (Romans 14:17) that the kingdom of God is neither food nor drink but righteousness, peace, and joy in the Holy Spirit. He tells the Ephesians to choose being filled with the Holy Spirit over the debauchery of getting drunk with wine (Ephesians 5:18).

So how on earth did wine come to represent, or according to the doctrine of transubstantiation actually become, the blood of Christ Jesus for Christians? This transformation of meaning did not happen overnight but emerged as Christianity became increasingly severed from its Jewish roots. You can see evidence of this in John's gospel, which has Jesus declare, "Those who eat my flesh and drink my blood have eternal life, and I will raise them up on the last day; for my flesh is true food and my blood is true drink. Those who eat my flesh and drink my blood abide in me, and I in them" (John 6:54–56).

Holy Communion as a Sacrament

As is the case with baptism, Holy Communion is a central feature of worship at all liturgical churches. The term "liturgy" is in fact used interchangeably with Holy Communion.[31] In addition, Christians pretty much agree that the rite we now consider a sacrament was instituted by Jesus during a Passover *seder* (order) as recorded in the synoptic gospels. During that meal, he took the unleavened bread, prayed a *berukah* over the bread, broke it and gave it to his disciples, telling them, "This is my body given for you; do this in remembrance of me" (Luke 22:19, NIV).

Toward the end of the seder, he recited, as practice dictated, a berukah over the last cup of wine. He offered the cup to his disciples, telling them, "This cup is the new covenant in my blood, which is poured out for you" (Luke 22:20, NIV). And as was the case with baptism, disputes about communion emerged. As Christianity became formalized as a separate religion, church authorities raised questions about:

- *What is Holy Communion?* Are bread and wine changed into the actual body and blood of Christ? Does the body and blood of Christ exist whole and unchanged in bread and wine? Do bread and wine represent the body and blood of Christ? What does "real presence" actually mean?

- *What does Holy Communion involve?* Bread and wine always? Always bread but sometimes wine? Does the wine always have to be red? May unfermented grape juice be substituted for wine? Must bread be unleavened and if so, must it be made of wheat?

- *What sort of preparation is required?* For how long should recipients fast before receiving Holy Communion? Must Holy Communion be preceded by a rite of penance?

- *Who may distribute communion?* Ordained clergy or commissioned ministers only? May any baptized Christian distribute communion if the host has already been consecrated?

- *How must communion be received?* Standing? Kneeling? On the tongue? In the hands? With the head bowed and without making eye contact? May the host be dipped into the wine? And how many times a year must it be received?

- *Where should communion take place?* In a church sanctuary only and at every service? At home? Wherever two or more are gathered in the name of Christ Jesus?

For Jewish followers of Jesus, these issues simply didn't exist. How on earth could they? At a Passover seder on the night before he died, Jesus poignantly instructed his disciples to break bread in his memory. He asked them to think differently about the seder's final, fourth cup of wine signifying hope and redemption. Earlier in his ministry he taught about the power of fellowship, about the power of his presence whenever two or more gathered together in his name (Matthew 18:19–20). He modeled inclusivity by eating with tax collectors and sinners (Matthew 9:9–11, 26:6; Mark 14:3;

Luke 5:27–32, 7:34, 19:1–10). And so, the night before he died, Jesus asked his disciples to remember him and everything he taught whenever they congregated. It was common for believers to congregate.

The Pharisees had already established *chavurot* (fellowships) to provide mutual support for religious observance. Followers of Jesus simply developed, while he was still alive, yet another *chavurah* to supplement Temple worship.[32] After his death and resurrection, Jesus' followers continued gathering in homes for prayer, study, and table celebrations. As for the table celebrations, you might imagine these as somewhat riotous meals filled with laughter and joy. Indeed, one Greek word for love, *agape*, was used to characterize these gatherings. The Christ had appeared! Some followers had only met him as Jesus of Nazareth, others had encountered him risen indeed. There were stories to tell and retell, miracles to praise and proclaim. Why on earth would they gather in somber silence?

In addition, members of this new chavurah sold their possessions, distributed the proceeds, and pooled resources (Acts 2:42–47; 4:32–35). Followers of The Way were more engaged in building a community than developing an elaborate theology of sacrifice. The early disciples preached the good news of death vanquished, the kingdom of God glimpsed (Acts 2:22–28). Resurrection of the dead, a belief many Jews already held, was shown to be true: eternal life was more than a promise. Why on earth would they live in fearful isolation from other believers?

Around 55 C.E., Paul preached that righteousness, previously obtained by following God's commandments, could now be achieved through faith in Jesus as Christ (Romans 3:21–26). As Christ, Jesus was the ultimate sacrifice of atonement for all sin (Romans 3:25) and a fragrant offering to God (Ephesians 5:2).

Writing in the late 60s C.E., the author of Hebrews amplified the notion of sacrifice. Jesus was the greatest of great high priests offering himself as gift and sacrifice (Hebrews 2:17; Hebrews 4:14–5:10). This emerging belief developed spiritual momentum and force after sacrificial worship and the priesthood were eliminated along with the Second Temple. Again, you can see evidence for this in John's gospel, which has the Last Supper taking place just before the Passover Feast (John 13:1). Jesus is the sacrificial lamb at that meal, which is not, in this gospel, a Passover seder. Nevertheless, centuries passed before Christian religious authorities created a formal liturgy that recalled Jesus' self-sacrifice as the lamb of God.

The doctrine of transubstantiation emerged over time. The concept of "transubstantiation," formally articulated by Thomas Aquinas during the thirteen century, was established as church dogma for the first time during the Fourth Lateran Council in 1215. (This was also the church council directing secular rulers to force Jews to identify themselves by wearing yellow badges and empowering Dominicans to preach in Jewish synagogues on Shabbat, something that continued in Rome until the seventeenth century.) Transubstantiation is the belief that bread and wine are completely changed into the body and blood of Christ. In the Roman Catholic Church, this substantive change happens when the priest, acting in the role of Christ, consecrates bread and wine.

Doctrinal challenges emerging during the fourteenth century were brought to a head by Luther during the sixteenth century. Luther argued that instead of being turned into body and blood, bread and wine co-existed whole and unchanged "in, with, and under" the consecrated bread and wine (i.e., consubstantiation). Christ was truly if not "really" present. Luther also taught that anyone, even scoundrels and sinners, could take Holy Communion and obtain the redemptive benefits of doing so.

Around the same time, Ulrich Zwingli suggested everyone get a grip and understand that scripture references to, and church rituals dealing with, the body and blood of Christ were symbolic.[33] Zwingli's argument was met with horror by some, relief by others. As someone raised Jewish, I can easily imagine what European Jews thought of all this, especially since blood libels had already become a fierce excuse for anti-Jewish violence.

Blood Libels

That blood libels have persisted throughout history underscores Christian ignorance about how clearly Torah law prohibits contact with, let alone consumption of, blood.

Blood libels are the accusation that Jews slaughter Christian boys and use their blood to bake *matzoh* (unleavened bread) for Passover. For centuries, this obscene misinterpretation of Exodus 12:13 relative to Eucharistic prayers was used to justify torturing and murdering Jews. Blood libels emerged as early as the second century C.E. and gathered punitive momentum during the twelfth century.

Hard to believe that variations on the theme of Jewish blood lust are still trotted out in some parts of the world today, but they are.

Fast forward to the twenty-first century and while Roman Catholics, Lutherans, and Anglican/Episcopalians do not fully agree about when and how Christ becomes present, the structure of our Holy Communion rites are highly congruent. The sequence of rituals for preparing the Lord's table is basically the same among these churches and replicates much of the Jewish liturgy (see also Chapter 3: Worship).

During the preparation of the altar, the celebrant prays *berakot* (benedictions) over bread and wine: "Blessed are you, Lord, God of all creation. Through your goodness we have this bread to offer, which earth has given and human hands have made . . ." and "Blessed are you, Lord, God of all creation. Through your goodness we have this wine to offer, fruit of the vine and work of human hands."

From the perspective of Judaism, the eucharistic prayer is also a berakah: "Father, all-powerful and ever-living God, we do well always and everywhere to give you thanks . . ."[34] or "God of all power, Ruler of the Universe, you are worthy of glory and praise . . ."[35]

The chavurah is invited to proclaim God's glory by praying *kodosh, kodosh, kodosh*: "Holy, holy, holy Lord, God of power and might, heaven and earth are full of your glory. Hosanna in the highest . . ." At this point in the rite, Christian believers split along denominational lines, although there has been movement toward "full communion" allowing Christians to receive communion at one another's worship services. The Evangelical Lutheran Church of America and the Episcopal Church reached an agreement about full communion in 2001.[36]

Currently, the Roman Catholic Church is in full communion with only the Eastern Orthodox churches. During the late 1960s, a formal Lutheran-Catholic dialogue resulted in some agreement about the Eucharist as a sacrifice and the presence of Christ in the Lord's Supper, affirmed persisting disagreements about other points, and ended with a plea that "fellow Lutherans and Catholics . . . examine their consciences and root out many ways of thinking, speaking and acting, both individually and as churches, which have obscured their unity in Christ on these as on many other matters.[37] But note how by

1999, the Lutheran World Federation and the Roman Catholic Church reached an agreement about the doctrine of justification,[38] so who can say when and how the Holy Spirit will move among contemporary Christian believers? Regarded through the lens of Judaism, these disputes are as perplexing today as they probably would have been to early followers of The Way who, as we know, came together as *chavarim* (fellows/friends) to celebrate the Lord's Supper.

After the last seder, Jesus' followers continued doing what they'd always done—they observed washing rituals before blessing bread and eating it; they blessed wine before drinking it, only now doing so in conscious remembrance of the risen Lord. They continued a long-standing tradition of hospitality, radicalizing it by extending table fellowship to Gentiles and pagans. At that point in our shared Jewish history, all were truly and really welcome to share bread and wine as one body by virtue of having been baptized by one Spirit (1 Corinthians 12:13).

Table Fellowships I Have Known

Like many of my restless generation, I sought community during my youth. My college sorority was one of the first ways this was manifested, and looking back, I can see the role table fellowship played. Sisterhood was mighty powerful at meals.

Never one to miss a counter-cultural trend, I logged time at one Hindu ashram during the early 1970s and then another during the late 1980s. Table fellowship in those determinedly spiritual environments frequently involved maintaining silence and staring transcendently into middle distance.

Every community I've ever participated in has taught me about the soul-nourishing value of table fellowship, whether coming to the table meant being there in silence or high-spirited chatter. I also learned the importance of bussing my own dishes and can run an institutional-sized dishwasher. These skills came in handy when I shifted to visiting Christian monasteries and retreat centers.

Last Supper as Last Seder

Every once in a while I encounter a Christian who doesn't realize the Last Supper was a Passover seder. I find this weird. Even more disconcerting is running into a brother or sister in Christ who doesn't know much about Passover at all! I believe Christians need to have detailed knowledge about Passover, so let me provide some.

One of the appointed feasts of the Lord according to the Torah, Passover (a.k.a. The Feast of Unleavened Bread) commemorates the Israelites' deliverance from Egypt (Exodus 12:1–13:16). Each spring, during a ceremonial meal, Jews everywhere remember and celebrate being protected from death by the blood of a lamb, baking unleavened bread for sustenance, the hurried flight from Egyptian slavery, and safe escape through the Sea of Reeds. The timing (i.e., 14 Nisan); place (i.e., at table), preparation (i.e., specific food, ceremonial washing), and manner (i.e., retelling the story) for this ceremonial meal is set forth in the Torah (Exodus 12:1–20; Numbers 9:11–12; Deuteronomy 16:1–8).

Passover has always been a big deal holiday and the joyous frenzy of preparation isn't conveyed in the synoptic gospels (Matthew 26:17–19; Mark 14:12–16; Luke 22:7–13). We aren't told exactly how some disciples went to the Temple to buy a male lamb "without blemish" for the holiday meal. We aren't given details about other disciples dashing around Jerusalem gathering spring greens, bitter herbs, nuts, dried fruits, honey, rice, and grain to bake into matzoh. We certainly aren't told how they brought these festive fixings back to the upper room so that (probably) the faithful women could prepare the meal of liberation.

Once gathered at table, everyone would have lifted hands and hearts up to the Lord with thanks and praise, blessing God always and everywhere for many gifts. Here are just a few of those prayers:

- *Blessed are You, O Lord our God, King of the Universe, who has given us life, sustained us, and brought us to this celebration.*

- *Blessed are You, O Lord our God, King of the Universe, who creates the fruit of the vine.*

- *Blessed are You, O Lord our God, King of the Universe, who has commanded us to eat unleavened bread.*

- *Blessed are You, O Lord our God, King of the Universe, who has commanded us to eat bitter herbs.*

- *Blessed are You, O Lord our God, King of the Universe, for the earth and its sustenance.*

- *Blessed are You, O Lord our God, King of the Universe, you have made us to be free.*

Not only are these benedictions still prayed during Passover seders, but their legacy lives on in the Eucharistic prayer during liturgy and Christian table prayers (i.e., grace) before and after meals.

All Jewish blessings begin with: "Blessed are You, O Lord our God, King of the Universe, who has . . ." All blessings continue by zooming in on something revealing God's generosity and acknowledging our responsibility to thank God. All blessings end with an invitation to say "Amen." Observant Jews are required, by tradition, to recite one hundred *berakot* every day not as an accountability exercise, but as a way of expressing gratitude for God's creation. Seems like a lot? Not if you believe in God's sovereignty everywhere and in everything.[39]

About My First Holy Communion

Of these features of my First Holy Communion you can be very sure: I did not dress up like a mini-bride. I did not walk down the center aisle of a church with my hands pressed together in prayer position. My proud parents were not standing on either side of me as I approached the altar. I hadn't prepared by telling a priest how I'd been mean to my little brother.

Looking back, I realize that the scenario for my FHC was remarkably close to a first-century experience of The Way. I attended a home-based gathering of Christian believers. We prayed. We sang. We broke matzoh in remembrance of Our Lord, Jesus the Christ and fed it to one another. I cried.

Even though I was baptized and attending Roman Catholic Mass, I did not receive communion. I'd read the fine print in the missal and knew I wasn't allowed to receive communion because I hadn't been confirmed in the Roman Catholic Church. For a while, I contented myself with reciting "we acknowledge one baptism" part of the Nicene Creed somewhat loudly.

After three (I'm not making this up) years of not receiving the Eucharist during Mass, I found myself being quizzed about this by a religious sister. We were at a week-long retreat. She knew I was born and raised Jewish. She knew I was baptized. She wanted to know why I wasn't receiving communion. "I'm following the rules," I said, pointing to the fine print. "Receive communion," she replied, with a deep sigh. After that, I did.

Holy Communion Timeline
(Common Era)

———

c. 95   Term "Eucharist" used for service of the Lord's Supper.

2nd–
3rd c.   "Real Presence" accepted as a concept.

          Holy Communion celebration on Sunday nearly universal.

3rd c.   Holy Communion must be received at Christmas, Easter, and Pentecost.

          Holy Communion must be celebrated on an altar.

4th c.   Communicants must fast before receiving Holy Communion (Synod of Hippo).

5th c.   Roman Rite established and term "Mass" popularized.

7th c.   Intinction (i.e., dipping bread into wine) common.

          Intinction forbidden (Third Council of Braga).

8th c.   Holy Communion in both kinds for laity begins disappearing from Western church.

11th c. Intinction becomes common.

          Aquinas articulates doctrine of transubstantiation.

12th c. Intinction forbidden (Council of Westminster).

          Practice begins of elevating Host during consecration.

13th c. Term "transubstantiation" becomes officially used (Twelfth Ecumenical Council).

          Holy Communion must be received at least once a year at Easter.

Laity not allowed to receive from the cup (Synod of Lambeth).

14th c. Wycliffe challenges and repudiates doctrine of transubstantiation.

15th c. Roman church formally declares Holy Communion a sacrament (Council of Florence).

16th c. Zwingli preaches Holy Communion one of two sacraments.

Luther asserts doctrine of consubstantiation.

Zwingli preaches that "body" and "blood" have symbolic meaning.

Roman church declares Christ instituted Holy Communion as one of seven sacraments, permits daily Eucharist, and reaffirms doctrine of transubstantiation (Council of Trent).

Roman church allows white wine for Holy Communion.

Book of Common Prayer abolishes mixing water with communion wine; insists Christians receive communion at least three times a year; and mandates people must kneel to receive communion (i.e., "Black Rubric").

Calvin repudiates transubstantiation.

"Black Rubric" removed from *Book of Common Prayer.*

19th c. Baptists allow all Christian believers to receive Holy Communion.

20th c. Roman church recommends daily Holy Communion for laity.

Patriarch of Constantinople calls for "mutual cooperation" among churches.

20th c.   Roman church allows laity to receive from the cup at Holy Communion.

Roman church allows Intinction.

Church of England allows other Christians to receive Holy Communion at Anglican churches.

Roman Catholic Church allows members of Orthodox Churches, Assyrian Church of the East, and the Polish National Catholic Church to receive Holy Communion. All other Christians must get permission from a bishop.

⸺⧼◎⧽⸺

FOR REFLECTION AND DISCUSSION

• How does knowing more about dietary laws set forth in the Torah change how you understand and appreciate Holy Communion?

• How does knowing that baptized Christians hold different beliefs about the nature and meaning of bread and wine affect your own beliefs about Holy Communion?

• Which features of chavurah are alive and well in your church community today? What needs to happen for this form of fellowship to emerge in and be sustained by your church community?

—◦/◦/◦—

TRY THIS

What, in practical terms, does it mean to welcome a stranger or see Christ in everyone? Meditate on these two passages, the first from Exodus and the second from the Rule of St. Benedict and then, consider how you might become more hospitable—in your life as well as at your table in your home.

"You shall not oppress a stranger; you know the heart of a stranger, for you were strangers in the land of Egypt . . ." (Exodus, 23:9, RSV).

"Let all guests who arrive be received like Christ, for He is going to say, 'I came as a guest, and you received Me' (Matthew 25:35). And to all let due honor be shown, especially to the domestics of the faith and to pilgrims. As soon as a guest is announced, therefore, let the Superior or the brethren meet him with all charitable service. . . . In the salutation of all guests, whether arriving or departing, let all humility be shown. Let the head be bowed or the whole body prostrated on the ground in adoration of Christ, who indeed is received in their persons. . . . Let the Abbot give the guests water for their hands; and let both Abbot and community wash the feet of all guests. After the washing of the feet let them say this verse: 'We have received Your mercy, O God, in the midst of Your temple' (Psalm 47:10)."[40]

CHAPTER SIX

Confirmation

Teach me to do your will, for you are my God;
let your good spirit lead me on a level path.

PSALM 143:10

Every human society has developed a set of activities marking the transition from one stage of life to another. Every religion has developed at least one ritual marking the transformation of individual believers into members of a faith community. Community creates ceremony and ceremony creates community. For Lutherans and Episcopalians, confirmation serves as that rite of passage. For Christians in the Roman Catholic and Eastern Orthodox churches, it's a sacrament of initiation. In either case, it's a ritual with complex connections to Judaism even though Judaism didn't have a confirmation ceremony until the nineteenth century.

Scripture tells us that as God's people, the Israelites were guided and inspired by the Holy Spirit for thousands of years before Jesus was born. A pillar of cloud by day and a pillar of fire by night led their escape from Egyptian bondage, guiding them on their journey to Canaan. God spoke with Moses face-to-face but was revealed in visions and spoke in dreams to prophets and priests. The prophet Samuel anointed Saul's head with oil and declared that "the spirit of the Lord will possess you, and you will be in a prophetic frenzy along with a procession of prophets and be turned into a different person" (1 Samuel 10:6). Still, you will not find within Judaism a special, specific ruach hakodesh. In fact, you'll also find references to the *shekhinah* (Holy Spirit) which refers to the feminine aspect of God in Judaism's Kabbalistic tradition. Coming into community involved learning and living according to Torah law. When, after nearly three millennia of existence, some Jewish movements developed a confirmation ceremony, it was to mark a rite of passage into community. As a result, I view confirmation through the lens of a religious tradition that anchors community responsibilities in God-given ethics.

Confirmation as Sacrament

Sacrament or not, confirmation simply wasn't a conceptual category for first-century Jews who came to believe Jesus was the Christ. Some had been around long enough to hear Jesus teaching. Some had personally been called to repentance and baptism by Peter during the Shavuot after the Ascension. Others had heard about the "sound like the rush of a violent wind" and its aftermath second or third hand (Acts 2:1–4). What happened?

Jerusalem was stressed and strange that year. Not only had Jesus been crucified by the Romans, but his inner circle of disciples claimed to have seen him fully alive, resurrected from the dead. Attempts to poke holes, literally and figuratively, only affirmed that reality. In the days following Passover, the risen Christ (because now he was surely the Christ) had appeared to continue teaching and counseling his devastated disciples. "Do not leave Jerusalem," he told them, "but wait for the gift my Father promised, which you have heard me speak about. For John baptized with water, but in a few days you will be baptized with the Holy Spirit"(Acts 1:4–5, NIV).

Of course they stayed. The Festival of Weeks known as Shavuot or Pentecost was coming up fifty days after Passover. They returned to the Great Temple to sacrifice their first sheaves of newly cut barley (the *omer*) (Leviticus 21:15–16, 21; Acts 2:5). They thanked God for the gift of Torah because by then Shavuot had been transformed from a spring harvest festival to a day with spiritual significance. Shavuot commemorated when God gave the Law to the Israelites on Mt. Sinai. In time, Pentecost would be celebrated by Christians as the birth of the Church, but at that point, Pentecost was Shavuot.

Confirmation was also not an issue because the concept of "sacrament"—never mind how many there were—wouldn't be defined until the early Middle Ages.[41] For Jewish followers of Jesus, water immersion, anointing with oil, and the laying on of hands were familiar rituals being put to new symbolic uses. To join The Way, they were baptized and blessed by the laying on of hands, just as Jesus had been baptized and just as he had blessed his disciples. Confirmation and baptism wouldn't become separate rites until 460 C.E. By then, Judaism and Christianity had long since parted ways.

By the eleventh century, the Eastern and Western churches, which had already split over doctrinal disputes in the Great Schism of 1054, nevertheless managed to agree about how to confer the Holy Spirit. They continued the venerable tradition of anointing with oil and the laying on of hands in the rite known as *Chrismation,* although they disagreed about the sequence of ritual actions.

In 1265, Thomas Aquinas argued that confirmation was a sacrament established by Christ, but the Roman Church wouldn't formally affirm it as one until the Council of Florence in 1438. Confirmation was re-declared a sacrament one hundred years later during the Council of Trent because, in part, the Protestant reformers had passionately argued that it was absolutely not. Today only the Eastern Orthodox and Roman Catholic churches consider confirmation a Sacrament of Initiation.

Come Holy Spirit

How might everyone gathered in the upper room have understood the significance of what happened during Pentecost? How long did it take them to realize the Holy Spirit was available to all believers, not just an exclusive group of elders?

I recommend rereading Luke's full account of the Pentecost event in the second chapter of Acts. When you've finished reading that, return to Hebrew scripture and contemplate these verses from Numbers: "[Moses] gathered seventy elders of the people, and placed them all around the tent. Then the Lord came down in the cloud and spoke to him, and took some of the spirit that was on him and put it on the seventy elders; and when the spirit rested upon them, they prophesied. But they did not do so again (Numbers 11:24–26).

Do you suppose anyone tapped Peter on the shoulder to remind him about this passage? How about Moses' wish that "all the Lord's people were prophets, and that the Lord would put his spirit on them" (Numbers 11:28–29), or his ability to confer the spirit of wisdom by the laying on of hands (Deuteronomy 34:9)?

Rite of Passage into Community

Early on during their efforts to reform Roman Catholicism, Luther in Germany and Zwingli in Switzerland set out to demote confirmation from its status as a sacrament. Neither of these Catholic scholars saw any valid scriptural basis for declaring it one. In his screed against practices of Rome, *The Babylonian Captivity of the Church*, Luther argued it was quite enough to view confirmation "as a certain churchly rite or sacramental ceremony, similar to other ceremonies, such as the blessing of water and the like."[42] The rite, he pointed out, was an historical development, a papist invention. It could, however, become valuable if confirmands focused on learning scripture. Otherwise, it was "monkey business" (*affenspiel*) and mumbo-jumbo (*gaukelwerk*). Preparation for this rite, said Luther, needed to be grounded in rigorous catechesis.

Splitting with Rome and establishing the Church of England meant King Henry VIII of England had to repudiate his previous defense of confirmation as a sacrament and side with rotestants who argued it was not.[43] Among Anglicans, confirmation was therefore considered a ceremony, albeit an important one during which confirmands would "express a mature commitment to Christ, and receive strength from the Holy Spirit through prayer and the laying on of hands by a bishop."[44] Despite arguing among themselves about the details of confirmation (e.g., proper age for this ceremony, which prayers and blessings to include, who may perform it), Protestants have generally agreed that Confirmation is not a sacrament and not a "completion" of Christian initiation.

Fast forward to the twenty-first century and you'll find Roman Catholics, Lutherans, and Episcopalians united in asserting confirmation is not a graduation from faith school. Instead, it marks—or it *should* mark—mature participation in Christian community. Sacrament or not, confirmation prep programs are structured accordingly. In these liturgical churches, candidates for confirmation must demonstrate their understanding of Christian precepts and denominationally specific practices. They need to understand and to affirm teachings of faith as articulated in both shared and denominationally specific creeds. Since confirmation happens within and is witnessed by community, preparation often includes community service.

Where is Judaism's influence in all this? As always, Judaism's legacy becomes visible once you know where and how to look for it. The first place to look is the *bar mitzvah* (son of commandment) ceremony which evolved over thousands of years into an important rite of passage into Jewish community.

Becoming a Bar Mitzvah

Jewish identity, which cannot be separated from community, is inextricably tied to living according to God's commandments (*mitzvot*) as recorded in the Torah. Jews have always been obligated to know what these commandments are as well as what they mean. Along with Judaism's central prayer, the *Shema* (Deuteronomy 6:4), the divine injunction to teach Torah appears in Deuteronomy:

> *And you shall love the Lord your God with all your heart, and with all your soul, and with all your might. And these words which I command you this day shall be upon your heart; and you shall teach them diligently to your children, and shall talk of them when you sit in your house, and when you walk by the way, and when you lie down, and when you rise. And you shall bind them as a sign upon your hand, and they shall be as frontlets between your eyes. And you shall write them on the doorposts of your house and on your gates. (Deuteronomy 6:5–9; RSV)*

Jesus of Nazareth emphasized how loving and serving God demanded this level of knowledge. When challenged by some Pharisees to identify the greatest among the 613 commandments, he answered like a Torah-savvy Jew, "You shall love the Lord your God with all your heart, and with all your soul, and with all your mind. This is the greatest and first commandment" (Matthew 22:37–38). He had already reassured his disciples and anyone listening in that entry into the kingdom of heaven depended on living according to Torah (Matthew 5:19–20). His mission, he said, was not to abolish but to fulfill the law. Until that is accomplished, "not one stroke of a letter, will pass from the law" (Matthew 5:17–18).

For many centuries before the Second Temple was destroyed, no formal ceremony was required to become a *bar mitzvah*. Could the boy read and understand the ethical, practical implications of Torah? If so, the obligation to be observant was conferred automatically. During Rabbinical Era, the ceremony was relatively (in every sense of the word) simple. On the first Shabbat service after his thirteenth birthday, the bar mitzvah had his first *aliyah* (going up) to chant the *berakot* (blessings) before and after the Torah reading, and then received a special blessing from the rabbi.

During the early Middle Ages, the synagogue ceremony expanded to involve more active and complex participation. And preparation! In addition to studying written law (Torah), the bar mitzvah needed to be conversant with rabbinical commentaries (Talmud). The *parashah* (Torah portion) and *haftarah* (writings of the prophets) had to be chanted in Hebrew. The bar mitzvah was required to demonstrate his interpretive competency by delivering a *drashah* or *Dvar Torah* (teaching or sermon), either during the ceremony or at the *Se'udah mitzvot* (festive meal) afterwards.

Community obligations and responsibilities also evolved. Over the centuries this rite of passage into Jewish adulthood would come to include a number of community-oriented rights. A son of the commandment counted toward a *minyan* (the quorum required for certain religious services). He had the right to lead religious services, form contracts, testify in religious courts and to marry, although the acceptable age for marriage had shifted upward by the fifteenth century. During the Middle Ages, the bar mitzvah was bound—literally—to Jewish teachings and traditions by the obligation to put on *tefillin* (phylacteries) during morning prayer.

As a Jewish rite of passage, the bar mitzvah ceremony has been as flexible as it has been durable. Historically, girls were not permitted to become a *bat mitzvah* (daughter of the commandment). This changed in 1922 when Conservative Rabbi Mordecai Kaplan ceremonially welcomed his daughter Judith into religious adulthood at his Manhattan synagogue. After World War II, the bat mitzvah ceremony became accepted, first among Conservative Jews in America and then among Reform Jews who had pretty much jettisoned the ceremony in favor of confirmation. Some Orthodox Jews finally embraced the bat mitzvah ceremony during the 1970s.

Did Jesus Have a Bar Mitzvah?

Those keen on arguing that Jesus had a bar mitzvah ceremony try to make their case by zooming in on Luke's gospel (Luke 2:41–52). You know the story and, if you're Catholic, you encounter it as one of the Joyful Mysteries when you pray the Rosary. This is the narrative about Joseph and Mary nearly making it all the way home from the annual Passover celebration in Jerusalem before realizing their twelve-year-old is missing. Where, pray tell, is Jesus?

They hauled themselves back to Jerusalem and searched for three days, only to find Jesus listening to and debating with teachers in the Great Temple. "Why the search?" he asked when his earthly parents arrived on the scene. "Couldn't you have figured out that I had to be in my Father's house?" The rabbis are amazed by this kid who knows Torah. (Perhaps they're also amazed that his frantic parents didn't spank him.)

Certainly this chronicle seems to have all the right features, but relying on it to make a case for Jesus having a bar mitzvah *ceremony* is problematic. For one thing, this ritual observance wasn't developed until after the Second Temple was destroyed. Perhaps Luke intentionally recorded this event in terms that first-century Jewish Christians could understand? After all, Jewish boys were encouraged to study Torah as soon as they could read. In fact, studying Torah was probably how they learned to read.

Did Jesus have a bar mitzvah?

I'm not convinced this is the right question and not because the answer tends to pit scholars and theologians against one another, which often gets ugly. The more accurate question is whether Jesus *was* a bar mitzvah. Since Jesus of Nazareth was an observant Jew who studied scripture, knew Jewish law, followed the mitzvot, and got into trouble for challenging religious and state authorities, I believe the answer is an unequivocal yes.

Did I Have a Bat Mitzvah?

Christians seem eager to know if I had a bat mitzvah ceremony. This question is usually popped right before asking, "What do your parents think about you being Catholic?" And they get to ask the second question pretty quickly because my short answer to the first one is, "no." My slightly longer answer is, "no way."

Understanding either version of my response requires knowing that well into the 1960s it was highly unusual for Jewish girls to have a bat mitzvah synagogue ceremony. And if we did, it absolutely did *not* involve a cocktail hour, videographer, chocolate fountain, and gifts more elaborate than a fountain pen or U.S. Savings Bond.

I've always assumed my family didn't view the bat mitzvah as authentically Jewish, which feels right when I recall the 1962 edition of my grandparents. My mother says I wanted no part of Hebrew school, which sounds right when I recall the 1962 edition of me.

As it turned out, I did make an appearance at the *bimah* to chant a blessing before one of the readings when my little brother became a bar mitzvah. I didn't expect the Torah scrolls to be so huge, even though I'd noticed my father staggering under their weight when the rabbi placed the scrolls in my father's arms. I didn't expect to feel odd about daring to touch the parchment, even though touching, embracing, and kissing the Torah is not only customary but expected.

I tell people that I finally allowed myself to be called to the Torah as a lector in the Roman Catholic Church. I cherish the transcendent but also very grounding privilege of reading holy scripture. I always struggle to resist a powerful urge to kiss the lectionary text, suspecting that if I did, everyone around me would plotz.

Confirmation and Contemporary Judaism

Shavuot's connection to the Sinai Covenant was highlighted even more when, during the nineteenth century, Reform Jews selected it to celebrate their newly established ceremony known as confirmation. Although it was intended as a way for teens to affirm Jewish identity, this ritual for boys and girls was opposed by Orthodox and Conservative Jews as being too Christian.

Jewish confirmation prep has always included learning Jewish beliefs, values, ethics, and history. It developed over time to include service and social justice projects to build community among the confirmands while teaching principles of *tzedakah* (the practice of righteousness) and *tikkun olam* (repairing the world). During a synagogue-based confirmation ceremony, confirmands lead the service, deliver the sermon, and make a public commitment to living a Jewish life.

Confirmation never did manage to replace the bar mitzvah ceremony either for the Reform Jews who originated it or the Conservative Jews who adopted it during the twentieth century. Nevertheless, in many Reform, Conservative, and Reconstructionist synagogues, confirmation has become meaningful, providing a solemn counterpoint as bar and bat mitzvah ceremonies continue devolving into extravagant parties.

About My Catholic Confirmation

I waited almost a decade between being baptized and seeking full communion with the Roman Catholic Church through the Sacrament of Confirmation. During that decade, I was literally driven to my knees with despair. I had to learn to walk by faith and not by fright, one day at a time and sometimes in even shorter increments. One particularly gruesome year included a trifecta of spiritual growth triggered by the death of my career, my marriage, and my father—in that order. The third person of the Trinity, the Holy Spirit, became a real presence in my messy little life. Thanks be to God.

It wasn't all bad, of course. The opening prayer for Compline, "God, come to my assistance. Lord, make haste to help me," was answered in unexpected delightful ways. I wrote and published three books. I sang. I sought and received church annulments for two marriages. I became enthralled with gardening. Friends showed up with food, clothing, major appliances. I soaked myself in scripture and warm baths. I painted a few icons and developed a thing for the Archangel Gabriel.

One Sunday, I sought out my deacon and said, "I believe my Easter is coming up this year." He grinned and hugged me. My priest wisely asked me to prepare by fasting from the Eucharist during that Lent, which ended up being more emotionally and spiritually difficult than I'd anticipated. I invited my mother to attend Easter Vigil. How would it be for her to watch a priest laying hands on her daughter's head? How would it be for her to hear all the "Christ our Lord" language during the rite? How would it be for her to see me receive the Eucharist and make the sign of the Cross? How would it be for me? Essential. So, I got myself confirmed as a Roman Catholic.

A year or so later, it dawned on me that I had no certificate and no one had asked if I wanted a confirmation name. When I complained about this, the priest (perhaps prophetically) quipped, "We're waiting to see if it works out."

Confirmation Timeline
(Common Era)

———

1st c. Some Jews become baptized and consider themselves followers of Christ Jesus.

3rd c. Baptism distinguished from the laying on of hands.

5th c. Confirmation becomes a separate rite.

9th c. Confirmation becomes a separate rite conferring the Holy Spirit.

15th c. Roman Church formally declares confirmation a sacrament (Council of Florence).

16th c. Luther and Zwingli say confirmation is not a sacrament, it's a rite, and that catechesis should be the focus of preparation.

Roman Church affirms that confirmation is a sacrament instituted by Christ (Council of Trent).

King Henry VIII of England says confirmation is a sacrament.

Early Lutheran Church asserts that confirmation is neither a sacrament nor a separate liturgical rite.

17th c. Church of England declares that confirmation is not a sacrament.

Eastern Orthodox and Roman Catholic churches assert that confirmation is a sacrament.

19th c. Reform Jews develop a rite of passage called confirmation.

Orthodox and Conservative Jews decry confirmation as too Christian.

20th c.   Conservative Jews agree that a confirmation rite that includes learning about Judaism makes sense.

Orthodox Jews reject Jewish confirmation.

Eastern Orthodox and Roman Catholic churches view confirmation as a sacrament of initiation.

The Lutheran Church views confirmation as an important rite of passage with catechesis as the focus of preparation.

Episcopal Church characterizes confirmation as "a rite in search of theology."

21st c.   Confirmation is a sacrament of initiation (Eastern Orthodox and Roman Catholic churches).

Confirmation is a rite of passage, and learning about faith should be the focus of preparation (Reform and Conservative Judaism, Lutheran Church, Anglican/Episcopal Church).

FOR REFLECTION AND DISCUSSION

- How does your understanding of and appreciation for confirmation change if you view it as a rite of passage? As a core sacrament?

- How do you define religious formation? How about spiritual formation? How would you determine anyone is ready to be confirmed? How does participating in a ceremony make a difference?

- What does it mean to become part of a community? How might this differ from becoming part of a faith community?

TRY THIS

The Book of Ruth, read during Shavuot, contains these beloved verses, "'Entreat me not to leave you or to return from following you; for where you go I will go, and where you lodge I will lodge; your people shall be my people, and your God my God'" (Ruth 1:16, RSV). Consider reading Ruth in its entirety during Pentecost, and notice how doing so might shape that holy day for you.

Afterword

Roller coaster, loop-de-loop, whirligig, teeter-totter, merry-go-round. Taken any of these thrill-n-chill rides lately? By the end of this book project, I felt as if I'd been on all of them multiple times and without much protective gear. I spent years preparing to write this book, years that included developing at least four different versions of the proposal for three different publishers. Still, the book shape-shifted once I started writing.

Once I started writing, my already intense interior life became unimaginably more so.

I found myself plunged into what Jungians call the "collective unconscious," which, for Jews, generally means accessing memories of diaspora and annihilation. Years of research and reading had gotten me so stuck in my head that I was unprepared for feeling such primal grief; not constantly, but frequently enough to raise questions I thought had long been answered.

"The problem with you," one special person regularly pointed out, "is that you're really a first-century Jewish follower of Jesus stuck in the twenty-first century." Sometimes I find this perspective comforting; at other times, not so much.

Thanks to a couple of international incidents, the part of my exterior life having to do with religion (as distinguished from my faith) became mighty uncomfortable during the time it took to write *Why Is There a Menorah On the Altar?*

Israel's bombing of Gaza in the winter of 2009 highlighted key differences in responses to that quick, brutal war within and between Christian and Jewish communities. I calibrated my conversation depending upon the type of Jew or type of Christian I was talking with until deciding to shut up about it altogether.

One month before this manuscript was due, I watched with nauseated horror as decades of Catholic-Jewish relations were nearly destroyed by the Vatican's initial misguided and mishandled welcome-back-to-the-fold outreach to a known Holocaust-denier. This also drove me nuts, and I confess to wondering whether other Jews were right to consider me a traitor to the tribe and Protestants right to consider me foolish, if not stupid, for being a big "c" Catholic. Nevertheless, the suggestion that I was not a "good" or at least good enough Catholic made me sob into the phone to sympathetic cradle Catholics and eventually consult with a canon lawyer. It was one thing for me to declare, "I've had enough," quite another to have anyone else question my fidelity.

My faith in the God of Israel and belief in Jesus as the Christ is what keeps me from tumbling irretrievably off the religion merry-go-round. So, too, does taking a long view that reaches back more than 5,700 years and continues forward on through eternity. All of it compels me to chant the Shema and the Lord's Prayer with equal fervor, to proclaim along with the psalmist:

> *Save us, O Lord our God, and gather us from*
> *among the nations,*
>
> *that we may give thanks to your holy name*
> *and glory in your praise.*
>
> *Blessed be the Lord, the God of Israel,*
> *from everlasting to everlasting.*

PSALM 106:47–48

Timeline: Christianity Emerges From Judaism[45]

We believe in one God,
the Father, the Almighty . . .

NICENE CREED

Note: Dates are approximate (circa/ca.)

B.C.E.

ca. 550–449
Pentateuch (Five Books of Moses) gains recognition as scripture.

ca. 260–250
Septuagint translation of the *Torah* into Greek.

ca. 200
Prophets (2nd major section of Hebrew scripture) recognized by some as scripture.

At the turn of the era
Jewish sages Hillel and Shammai head dominant and competing schools of Jewish thought and theology.

ca. 4–2
Yeshua (Jesus) of Nazareth is born.

C.E.

ca. 27
Jesus baptized by John the Baptist.

ca. 27–37
Jesus crucified.

ca. 33–34
Saul of Tarsus, a Pharisee and persecutor of Jewish
followers of Jesus, has his Damascus experience and
becomes a believer in Christ Jesus.

ca. 35–65
The Apostolic Age. Missionaries of this Jewish sect were
called "apostles"—those sent to teach the gospel (good
news) of Christ (in) Jesus.

ca. 37–100
Jewish historian Josephus lives and writes.

ca. 40
Followers of Jesus are first called "Christians."

ca. 48
Council of Jerusalem. Apostles and church elders meet
to debate whether Gentiles (non-Jews) can be Christians.
Must Gentile followers of Jesus keep Jewish law? Must
they be circumcised?

ca. 49
Peter and Paul part ways over whether Gentile followers
of Jesus must observe dietary laws when eating with
Jewish followers of Jesus. Christians expelled from Rome
by emperor Claudius.

ca. 50–125
Gospels of Mark, Matthew, and Luke written.

64
Peter crucified in Rome.

ca. 66
First Jewish War against Rome led by Zealots begins.

67
Paul beheaded in Rome.

70
Destruction of the Second Temple of Jerusalem ends priesthood, Temple sacrifice, and significantly changes debate about placing Christianity within or apart from Judaism.

74
First Jewish War against Rome ends with the fall of Masada.

75
Jewish followers of Jesus begin to be expelled from synagogues taking with them the norms, values, and practices that provide a foundation for Christian ethics and practice.

ca. 77
Josephus publishes *The War of the Jews.*

ca. 85
"Curse Against Heretics," aimed at Christians, added to Jewish synagogue benedictions. *Acts of the Apostles* completed.

ca. 90–150
Writings (3rd major section of Hebrew scripture) debated and accepted as sacred scripture.

ca. 90–110
Gospel of John written.

ca. 92
Christian communities begin evolving into churches governed by a single leader.

101
Early Christian rites rooted in Jewish liturgy established. Includes a cycle of daily prayers.

105
The term "Catholic" is applied to the church. Christianity still resembles Hellenistic Judaism.

ca. 114–117
Jewish revolts against Rome continue outside Palestine.

135
Establishment of Jerusalem as a pagan city and expulsion of Jews by Hadrian.

Glossary of Hebrew Terms and Jewish Concepts

Adonai
Hebrew: Lord. One common name for God, used especially during prayer.

Aliyah
Hebrew: going up. To "have an aliyah" means going up to the bimah to recite the blessing before the Torah reading.

Amidah
Central prayer of the Jewish worship service, recited silently while standing, also known as the *Shemoneh Esrai* or Eighteen Blessings.

Amud
Small desk or podium in the synagogue sanctuary from which services are led, if they're not led from the *bimah*.

Aron hakodesh
Hebrew: holy chest. Cabinet holding Torah scrolls, usually in the front of the sanctuary. Also referred to as the Ark, which is an acronym for aron hakodesh.

Ashkenazi
Jews from western and eastern Europe and their descendents.

Bar mitzvah
Hebrew: son of the commandment. Upon reaching age thirteen, a Jewish boy is expected to obey the commandments. Term also used for the ceremony marking this occasion.

Bat mitzvah
Hebrew: daughter of the commandment. Upon reaching age twelve, a Jewish girl is expected to obey the commandments. Term also used for the ceremony marking this occasion.

Bet Hillel
Hebrew: House of Hillel. Composed of those who followed first-century teacher and scholar Rabbi Hillel. Influenced the Pharisees, who were religious moderates.

Bet knesset
Hebrew: house of assembly. A function of synagogues.

Bet midrash
Hebrew: house of study. A function of synagogues.

Bet Shammai
Hebrew: House of Shammai. Composed of those who followed first-century teacher and scholar Rabbi Shammai. Influenced the Sadducees, who were religious fundamentalists.

Bet tefilah
Hebrew: house of prayer. A function of synagogues.

Ben
Hebrew: son of. Aramaic equivalent is "bar."

Berachah
Hebrew: blessing or benediction. Plural: *berakot*.

Bimah
Raised platform from which Torah is read and service is led.

Bris
Hebrew: covenant. Colloquial term for the ritual of circumcision, from the Ashkenazic pronunciation of *brit*.

Brit milah
Hebrew: covenant of circumcision. Circumcision ritual performed on the eighth day of a boy's life. More commonly known as *brit* or *bris*.

Challah
Portion of bread dough originally set aside for priests and then burned entirely as a sacrifice to God. Today, more commonly used to describe a braided loaf of bread used to celebrate the Sabbath.

Chanukiah
Special nine-branch candlestick used to celebrate Chanukah.

Chavurah
Hebrew: fellowships. Plural: *chavurot.*

Decalogue
The Ten Commandments.

Diaspora
Scattering of Jews to countries outside of Palestine after the Babylonian captivity. Lower-case usage (diaspora) refers to any group that has been dispersed or displaced from its homeland.

Haftarah
Hebrew: Concluding portion. Selection from the Prophets read during synagogue services on Shabbat and festivals after the Torah portion.

Halakhah
Hebrew: The Walk. Jewish Law, consisting of 613 mitzvot plus rabbinic law and custom.

Hashem
Hebrew: The Name. Used especially by Orthodox Jews to avoid saying a name of God.

Ketuvim
Hebrew: The Writings.

Kodesh/Kodosh
Hebrew: holy.

Kohanim
Hebrew: priests.

Kippah
Disc or beanie-like head covering. Known in Yiddish as a yarmulke.

Levites
Hebrew: associate priests.

Mappah
Hebrew: table covering. Covers the *bimah* in traditional synagogues.

Matzoh
Hebrew: unleavened bread. Unleavened (yeast-free) bread used during Passover based on Exodus 12:39. Also called the "bread of affliction" based on Deuteronomy 16:3.

Menorah
Hebrew: candelabrum. A seven-branch candlestick.

Mezuzah
Hebrew: doorpost. Small parchment of Torah verses placed on the doorpost of Jewish homes to fulfill the commandment of Deuteronomy 6:9.

Midrash
Hebrew: interpretation. Stories, sermons, parables, and other homiletic literature and exegesis.

Mikvah
Body of natural water used for ritual cleansing.

Minyan
Quorum of ten adult Jews required for complete public worship service and other observances.

Mishnah
Hebrew: teaching. According to traditional Jews, the oral Torah received by Moses at Sinai but not written down with rabbinic commentary until ca. 200 CE.

Mitzvah
Hebrew: commandment. Plural: mitzvot. Rules for religious action. Colloquially used to characterize any good deed.

Ner tamid
Hebrew: eternal light. Continuously burning lamp suspended in front of the ark

Nevi'im
Hebrew: Prophets. Second section of the Tanakh, including writings of the prophets and events covering approximately seven hundred years of Jewish history after Moses.

Omer
Literally a sheaf of wheat but also a unit of dry measurement approximately one gallon. The fifty-day period between Passover and Shavuot is known as "Counting of the Omer."

Parashah
Hebrew: portion. Torah portion assigned to a particular week or holy day.

Parochet
Hebrew: curtain. Placed in front of the ark holding the Torah scrolls.

Passover
Feast of Unleavened Bread commemorating Jewish deliverance from slavery in Egypt, as recounted in the biblical Book of Exodus.

Pentateuch
The Five Books of Moses (Genesis, Exodus, Leviticus, Numbers, Deuteronomy).

Rabbi
Hebrew: teacher.

Rosh Hashanah
Feast of Trumpets and the New Year according to the Hebrew calendar. An Appointed Feast of the Lord for Jews.

Ruach Hakodesh
Hebrew: Holy Spirit of God.

Sanhedrin
Religious court or council that included Pharisees and Sadducees.

Seder
Hebrew: Order. The Passover table service where the story of Exodus is recalled and special foods are eaten to commemorate redemption from slavery.

Sefer Torah
Handwritten Torah scroll kept in the Ark and read publicly on Shabbat, holidays, Mondays, and Thursdays.

Sephardic
Jews from the Middle East and Spain and their descendents.

Septuagint
Koine Greek translation of the Torah from Hebrew.

Se'udah mitzvot
Festive meal following the fulfillment of a mitzvah such as a circumcision or bar mitzvah ceremony.

Shabbat
Hebrew: Sabbath. Day of rest beginning Friday at sundown and concluding Saturday after sundown when three stars become visible. An Appointed Feast of the Lord for Jews.

Shavuot
Feast of Weeks. A spring grain festival and celebration of the Sinai Event, also known as Pentecost. An Appointed Feast of the Lord for Jews.

Shekhinah
Hebrew: Presence of God; the Holy Spirit. The feminine aspect of God according to Kabbalistic thought.

Shema
The central prayer of Judaism appearing in Deuteronomy 6:4.

Shemoneh Esrai
Hebrew: Eighteen Blessings. See: *Amidah*.

Siddur
Hebrew: Order. Plural: siddurim. Prayer book used for Jewish liturgy.

Sukkoth
Hebrew: Booths. Feast of Tabernacles. Eight-day autumn festival commemorating the Exodus and celebrating the harvest. An Appointed Feast of the Lord for Jews.

Tachanun
Penitential prayers prayed by observant Jews during morning worship.

Tallit
Hebrew: prayer shawl. The *tzitzit* (fringes) at the corners are aides for prayer.

Talmud
Hebrew: teaching. Rabbinic commentaries on the Torah, originally oral and then codified in writing.

Tanakh
Hebrew acronym for Torah (Five Books of Moses), Nevi'im (The Prophets), and Ketuvim (The Writings), which together constitute the Bible.

Tefillin
Phylacteries, small, black, leather cubes containing parchment inscribed with verses from Deuteronomy and Exodus. They're strapped to the left arm and forehead during weekday morning prayers by Orthodox and Conservative Jewish men, and some Conservative women.

Teshuvah
Hebrew: turning. Repentance; self-evaluation.

Tikkun olam
The obligation to participate in repairing the world; world peace; social justice.

Torah
Hebrew: Law. First five books of the Bible, also known as the Five Books of Moses or the Pentateuch. Alternative translation: instruction.

Tzedakah
Hebrew: righteousness. Ethical conduct; right relationship with God, all things, and all people. Colloquially used to characterize charitable giving.

Yahrzeit
Yiddish: anniversary. Annual anniversary of a loved one's death.

YHWH
Hebrew: I am or I will be. Sacred name of God revealed to Moses. Also known as the Tetragrammaton. Considered too holy to be pronounced, and usually replaced by Adonai (Lord) in Torah readings.

Yiddish
Combination of Middle High German, Hebrew, and Polish spoken and written by eastern European Jews and their descendents.

Yiddishkeit
Ways of being Jewish without necessarily being religious.

Yom Kippur
Day of Atonement observed ten days after Rosh Hashanah. An Appointed Feast of the Lord for Jews.

APPENDIX C

Selected Documents on Christian-Jewish Dialogue

Responding to another upsurge in anti-Semitism during the mid-1960s, the Episcopal Church (U.S.A.) and the Roman Catholic Church issued remarkable public statements that led the way to Christian-Jewish dialogue.

Deicide and the Jews (1964) and paragraph four of *Nostra Aetate* (1965) deplored anti-Semitism in general and, more specifically, the centuries-old charge that the Jewish people killed Jesus. In 1979, the Episcopal Church (U.S.A.) followed up with a resolution reaffirming the need for Episcopal-Jewish dialogue in light of this ongoing history of persecution. The Evangelical Lutheran Church in America issued a similar declaration in 1994.

As a more formal "Christian-Jewish Dialogue" emerged, it became clear that many Christian theologians, along with Christian clergy and religious, were as unschooled in Jewish history as they were in Jewish interpretations of scripture. Christian participants of these study groups became radicalized in the true sense of the word—they discovered their Jewish roots. They also discovered, or were finally able to see, evidence of what French historian Jules Isaac identified as the "teaching of Contempt."[46] As a result, the twenty-first century of the Common Era opened with a number of public statements about interfaith relations.

In 2000, *Dabru Emet: A Jewish Statement on Christians and Christianity* was crafted by scholars associated with the

Institute for Christian & Jewish Studies (ICJS). Two years later, The Christian Scholars Group on Christian-Jewish Relations issued *A Sacred Obligation: Rethinking Christian Faith in Relation to Judaism and the Jewish People*. Published essays followed, many of which revealed a high level of amazement and grief on the part of Roman Catholic, Lutheran, and Episcopal theologians and clergy—amazement about historical persistence of Christian arrogance and contempt toward Jews and Judaism; grief for the ways Judaism's legacy has been stripped from or ignored within Christian liturgical practice. And considerable dismay, dismay at their own complicity with anti-Jewish theology and liturgy.

Practical correctives have been somewhat slower in coming, especially those involving changes to the lectionary. Lutheran theologian Norman A. Beck has, for example, suggested Christians "avoid using the most hateful elements in the New Testament for private devotion and public worship," and called for "a revision of the lectionary that does not use the supersessionist and defamatory texts [during Holy Week and the Easter cycle]"[47] that has yet to happen.

In addition, there has been slippage around some important and necessary correctives. One example is the recent controversy around the Roman Catholic Latin liturgy for Good Friday, from which the prayer for the "faithless Jews" was removed by Pope John XXIII in 1959. While that exact language wasn't restored by Pope Benedict XVI in 2008, the Latin liturgy was revised so that it asks God to "enlighten" the hearts of the Jews so "they may acknowledge Jesus Christ, the savior of all men."[48] This has generated vigorous objections from Jewish leaders as well as interfaith theologians who take little comfort in the fact that the vast majority of American Catholics will continue hearing the prayer in its unchanged 1970 modern English version. And so it has been and so it goes.

Deicide and the Jews

1964 General Convention of the Episcopal Church (U.S.A.)[49]

Whereas, Within the Church, throughout the centuries, love-less attitudes including the charge of deicide, have frequently resulted in persecution of the Jewish people and a concomitant revulsion on the part of the Jewish people towards the un-Christ-like witness thus made; and

Whereas, Obedience to the Lord of the Church requires an honest and clear expression of love for our neighbour; and

Whereas, Persecution of the Jews has been recently intensified in certain areas of the world; and

Whereas, Lack of communication between Christians and Jews, and the resulting ignorance and suspicion of each other, has been a barrier to Christian obedience of the Law of Love; be it

Resolved, the House of Bishops concurring, That the General Convention of the Protestant Episcopal Church in the United States of America, meeting in St. Louis in October, 1964, reject the charge of deicide against the Jews and condemn anti-Semitism; and be it further

Resolved, the House of Bishops concurring, That the General Convention condemn unchristian accusations against the Jews; and that this Church seek positive dialogue with appropriate representative bodies of the Jewish Faith; and be it further

Resolved, the House of Bishops concurring, That the substance of this Resolution be referred to the Joint Commission on Ecumenical Relations for continuing study and suggested implementation.

Declaration on the Relation of the Church to Non-Christian Religions Nostra Aetate[50]

Proclaimed by His Holiness Pope Paul VI on October 28, 1965

(No. 4)

As the sacred synod searches into the mystery of the Church, it remembers the bond that spiritually ties the people of the New Covenant to Abraham's stock.

Thus the Church of Christ acknowledges that, according to God's saving design, the beginnings of her faith and her election are found already among the Patriarchs, Moses and the prophets. She professes that all who believe in Christ— Abraham's sons according to faith (6)—are included in the same Patriarch's call, and likewise that the salvation of the Church is mysteriously foreshadowed by the chosen people's exodus from the land of bondage. The Church, therefore, cannot forget that she received the revelation of the Old Testament through the people with whom God in His inexpressible mercy concluded the Ancient Covenant. Nor can she forget that she draws sustenance from the root of that well-cultivated olive tree onto which have been grafted the wild shoots, the Gentiles.(7) Indeed, the Church believes that by His cross Christ, Our Peace, reconciled Jews and Gentiles, making both one in Himself.(8)

The Church keeps ever in mind the words of the Apostle about his kinsmen: "theirs is the sonship and the glory and the covenants and the law and the worship and the promises; theirs are the fathers and from them is the Christ according to the flesh" (Rom. 9:4–5), the Son of the Virgin Mary. She also recalls that the Apostles, the Church's main-stay and pillars, as well as most of the early disciples who proclaimed Christ's Gospel to the world, sprang from the Jewish people.

As Holy Scripture testifies, Jerusalem did not recognize the time of her visitation,(9) nor did the Jews in large number, accept the Gospel; indeed not a few opposed its spreading.(10) Nevertheless, God holds the Jews most dear for the sake of their Fathers; He does not repent of the gifts He makes or of the calls He issues—such is the witness of the Apostle.(11) In company with the Prophets and the same Apostle, the Church awaits that day, known to God alone, on which all peoples will address the Lord in a single voice and "serve him shoulder to shoulder" (Soph. 3:9).(12)

Since the spiritual patrimony common to Christians and Jews is thus so great, this sacred synod wants to foster and recommend that mutual understanding and respect which is the fruit, above all, of biblical and theological studies as well as of fraternal dialogues.

True, the Jewish authorities and those who followed their lead pressed for the death of Christ;(13) still, what happened in His passion cannot be charged against all the Jews, without distinction, then alive, nor against the Jews of today. Although the Church is the new people of God, the Jews should not be presented as rejected or accursed by God, as if this followed from the Holy Scriptures. All should see to it, then, that in catechetical work or in the preaching of the word of God they do not teach anything that does not conform to the truth of the Gospel and the spirit of Christ.

Furthermore, in her rejection of every persecution against any man, the Church, mindful of the patrimony she shares with the Jews and moved not by political reasons but by the Gospel's spiritual love, decries hatred, persecutions, displays of anti-Semitism, directed against Jews at any time and by anyone.

Besides, as the Church has always held and holds now, Christ underwent His passion and death freely, because of the sins of men and out of infinite love, in order that all may reach salvation. It is, therefore, the burden of the Church's preaching to proclaim the cross of Christ as the sign of God's all-embracing love and as the fountain from which every grace flows.

Notes

6. Cf. *Gal.* 3:7

7. Cf. *Rom.* 11:17–24

8. Cf. *Eph.* 2:14–16

9. Cf. *Lk.* 19:44

10. Cf. *Rom.* 11:28

11. Cf. *Rom.* 11:28–29; cf. dogmatic Constitution, *Lumen Gentium* (Light of nations) AAS, 57 (1965) pag. 20

12. Cf. *Is.* 66:23; *Ps.* 65:4; *Rom.* 11:11–32

13. Cf. *John.* 19:6

Christian-Jewish Dialogue

A Resolution of the 1979 General Convention of the Episcopal Church (U.S.A.)

Whereas, the Church is reminded of all parts of the Holy Scripture of those spiritual ties which link the community of the New Testament to the seed of Abraham and is exhorted by St. Paul to recall that she is nourished by root and sap of that good and consecrated olive tree onto which the wild olive branches of the Gentiles have been grafted (Romans 11:17–24); and

Whereas, the Church cannot forget that she has received the revelation of the Old Testament from that people with whom God, in his infinite goodness and mercy, established and nourished those ancient covenants; and that St. Paul bears witness that the Jews remain precious to God for the sake of the patriarchs, since God does not withdraw the gifts he has bestowed or revoke the choices he has made (Romans 11:28–29); and

Whereas, our Lord Jesus Christ was born, circumcised, dedicated, and baptized into the community of Israel, to whom belong the sonship, the glory, the covenants, the giving of the Torah, the worship and the patriarchs (Romans 9:4–5): and the first apostles and witnesses themselves were all of Jewish lineage; and

Whereas, all the faithful in Christ consider themselves to be the offspring of Abraham (Galatians 3:7) and included in his call, being also the inheritors of that redemption figured in the Exodus of God's chosen people from bondage to Pharaoh; and

Whereas, Christian and Jew share the common hope for that day in which our God will be King over the whole earth (Zechariah 14:9) and, receiving the kingdom, will be "all in all" (I Corinthians 15:28), and are thus bound by that hope to a common divine service; and

Whereas, a denial of or an ignorance of their spiritual roots by Christians has, more often than not, provided fertile ground for the festering of antisemitism even among leaders of the Church of Jesus Christ—the Holocaust in Hitler's Germany being only the most recent and painful memory; therefore be it

Resolved, the House of Deputies concurring, That this 66th General Convention of the Episcopal Church call anew upon the leadership of the Episcopal Church, both clergy and lay, to deepen their commitment to Episcopal-Jewish dialogue and to interfaith cooperation in local communities; and, wherever appropriate, to seek exposure to ancient and contemporary Jewish scholarship so as to better comprehend the Scriptures on which, and the religious environment in which, our Lord Jesus Christ was nourished; and to appreciate more fully the religious worship and experience of our neighbors in the Jewish community; and be it further

Resolved, That, to the end of encouraging and furthering mutual understanding between Episcopalians and Jews by way of biblical and theological inquiry and through friendly discussion, the Presiding Bishop's Advisory Committee on Episcopal-Jewish Relations initiate a study on the methodology for and substantive issues of Episcopal-Jewish dialogue in the next triennium; and be it further

Resolved, That the report of the said Presiding Bishop's Advisory Committee on Episcopal-Jewish Relations, together with recommendations for implementation of the dialogue, be made to the 67th General Convention of the Episcopal Church.

Declaration of the Evangelical Lutheran Church in America to the Jewish Community[51]

The Church Council of the Evangelical Lutheran Church in America on April 18, 1994, adopted the following document as a statement on Lutheran-Jewish relations:

In the long history of Christianity there exists no more tragic development than the treatment accorded the Jewish people on the part of Christian believers. Very few Christian communities of faith were able to escape the contagion of anti-Judaism and its modern successor, anti-Semitism. Lutherans belonging to the Lutheran World Federation and the Evangelical Lutheran Church in America feel a special burden in this regard because of certain elements in the legacy of the reformer Martin Luther and the catastrophes, including the Holocaust of the twentieth century, suffered by Jews in places where the Lutheran churches were strongly represented.

The Lutheran communion of faith is linked by name and heritage to the memory of Martin Luther, teacher and reformer. Honoring his name in our own, we recall his bold stand for truth, his earthy and sublime words of wisdom, and above all his witness to God's saving Word. Luther proclaimed a gospel for people as we really are, bidding us to trust a grace sufficient to reach our deepest shames and address the most tragic truths.

In the spirit of that truth-telling, we who bear his name and heritage must with pain acknowledge also Luther's anti-Judaic diatribes and the violent recommendations of his later writings against the Jews. As did many of Luther's own companions in the sixteenth century, we reject this violent invective, and yet more do we express our deep and abiding sorrow over its tragic effects on subsequent generations. In concert with the Lutheran World Federation, we particularly deplore the appropriation of Luther's words by modern anti-Semites for the teaching of hatred toward Judaism or toward the Jewish people in our day.

Grieving the complicity of our own tradition within this history of hatred, moreover, we express our urgent desire to live out our faith in Jesus Christ with love and respect for the Jewish people. We recognize in anti-Semitism a contradiction and an affront to the Gospel, a violation of our hope and calling, and we pledge this church to oppose the deadly working of such bigotry, both within our own circles and in the society around us. Finally, we pray for the continued blessing of the Blessed One upon the increasing cooperation and understanding between Lutheran Christians and the Jewish community.

Dabru Emet: A Jewish Statement on Christians and Christianity[52]

In recent years, there has been a dramatic and unprecedented shift in Jewish and Christian relations. Throughout the nearly two millennia of Jewish exile, Christians have tended to characterize Judaism as a failed religion or, at best, a religion that prepared the way for, and is completed in, Christianity. In the decades since the Holocaust, however, Christianity has changed dramatically. An increasing number of official Church bodies, both Roman Catholic and Protestant, have made public statements of their remorse about Christian mistreatment of Jews and Judaism. These statements have declared, furthermore, that Christian teaching and preaching can and must be reformed so that they acknowledge God's enduring covenant with the Jewish people and celebrate the contribution of Judaism to world civilization and to Christian faith itself.

We believe these changes merit a thoughtful Jewish response. Speaking only for ourselves—an interdenominational group of Jewish scholars—we believe it is time for Jews to learn about the efforts of Christians to honor Judaism. We believe it is time for Jews to reflect on what Judaism may now say about Christianity. As a first step, we offer eight brief statements about how Jews and Christians may relate to one another.

Jews and Christians worship the same God. Before the rise of Christianity, Jews were the only worshippers of the God of Israel. But Christians also worship the God of Abraham, Isaac, and Jacob; creator of heaven and earth. While Christian worship is not a viable religious choice for Jews, as Jewish theologians we rejoice that, through Christianity, hundreds of millions of people have entered into relationship with the God of Israel.

Jews and Christians seek authority from the same book—the Bible (what Jews call "Tanakh" and Christians call the "Old Testament"). Turning to it for religious orientation, spiritual enrichment, and communal education, we each take away similar lessons: God created and sustains the universe; God established a covenant with the people Israel, God's revealed word guides Israel to a life of righteousness; and God will ultimately redeem Israel and the whole world. Yet, Jews and Christians interpret the Bible differently on many points. Such differences must always be respected.

Christians can respect the claim of the Jewish people upon the land of Israel. The most important event for Jews since the Holocaust has been the reestablishment of a Jewish state in the Promised Land. As members of a biblically based religion, Christians appreciate that Israel was promised—and given—to Jews as the physical center of the covenant between them and God. Many Christians support the State of Israel for reasons far more profound than mere politics. As Jews, we applaud this support. We also recognize that Jewish tradition mandates justice for all non-Jews who reside in a Jewish state.

Jews and Christians accept the moral principles of Torah. Central to the moral principles of Torah is the inalienable sanctity and dignity of every human being. All of us were created in the image of God. This shared moral emphasis can be the basis of an improved relationship between our two communities. It can also be the basis of a powerful witness to all humanity for improving the lives of our fellow human beings and for standing against the immoralities and idolatries that harm and degrade us. Such witness is especially needed after the unprecedented horrors of the past century.

Nazism was not a Christian phenomenon. Without the long history of Christian anti-Judaism and Christian violence against Jews, Nazi ideology could not have taken hold nor could it have been carried out. Too many Christians participated in, or were sympathetic to, Nazi atrocities against Jews. Other Christians did not protest sufficiently against these atrocities. But Nazism itself was not an inevitable outcome of Christianity. If the Nazi extermination of the Jews had been fully successful, it would have turned its murderous rage more directly to Christians. We recognize with gratitude those Christians who risked or sacrificed their lives to save Jews during the Nazi regime. With that in mind, we encourage the continuation of recent efforts in Christian theology to repudiate unequivocally contempt of Judaism and the Jewish people. We applaud those Christians who reject this teaching of contempt, and we do not blame them for the sins committed by their ancestors.

The humanly irreconcilable difference between Jews and Christians will not be settled until God redeems the entire world as promised in Scripture. Christians know and serve God through Jesus Christ and the Christian tradition. Jews know and serve God through Torah and the Jewish tradition. That difference will not be settled by one community insisting that it has interpreted Scripture more accurately than the other; nor by exercising political power over the other. Jews can respect Christians' faithfulness to their revelation just as we expect Christians to respect our faithfulness to our revelation. Neither Jew nor Christian should be pressed into affirming the teaching of the other community.

A new relationship between Jews and Christians will not weaken Jewish practice. An improved relationship will not accelerate the cultural and religious assimilation that Jews rightly fear. It will not change traditional Jewish forms of worship, nor increase intermarriage between Jews and non-Jews, nor persuade more Jews to convert to Christianity, nor create a false blending of Judaism and Christianity. We respect Christianity as a faith that originated within Judaism and that still has significant contacts with it. We do not see it as an extension of Judaism. Only if we cherish our own traditions can we pursue this relationship with integrity.

Jews and Christians must work together for justice and peace. Jews and Christians, each in their own way, recognize the unredeemed state of the world as reflected in the persistence of persecution, poverty, and human degradation and misery. Although justice and peace are finally God's, our joint efforts, together with those of other faith communities, will help bring the kingdom of God for which we hope and long. Separately and together, we must work to bring justice and peace to our world. In this enterprise, we are guided by the vision of the prophets of Israel:

> It shall come to pass in the end of days that the mountain of the Lord's house shall be established at the top of the mountains and be exalted above the hills, and the nations shall flow unto it . . . and many peoples shall go and say, "Come ye and let us go up to the mountain of the Lord to the house of the God of Jacob and He will teach us of His ways and we will walk in his paths." (Isaiah 2:2–3)

A Sacred Obligation:

Rethinking Christian Faith in Relation to Judaism and the Jewish People[53]

A Statement by The Christian Scholars Group on Christian-Jewish Relations

September 1, 2002

Since its inception in 1969, the Christian Scholars Group has been seeking to develop more adequate Christian theologies of the church's relationship to Judaism and the Jewish people. Pursuing this work for over three decades under varied sponsorship, members of our association of Protestant and Roman Catholic biblical scholars, historians, and theologians have published many volumes on Christian-Jewish relations.

Our work has a historical context. For most of the past two thousand years, Christians have erroneously portrayed Jews as unfaithful, holding them collectively responsible for the death of Jesus and therefore accursed by God. In agreement with many official Christian declarations, we reject this accusation as historically false and theologically invalid. It suggests that God can be unfaithful to the eternal covenant with the Jewish people. We acknowledge with shame the suffering this distorted portrayal has brought upon the Jewish people. We repent of this teaching of contempt. Our repentance requires us to build a new teaching of respect. This task is important at any time, but the deadly crisis in the Middle East and the frightening resurgence of antisemitism worldwide give it particular urgency.

We believe that revising Christian teaching about Judaism and the Jewish people is a central and indispensable obligation of theology in our time. It is essential that Christianity both understand and represent Judaism accurately, not only as a matter of justice for the Jewish people, but also for the integrity of Christian faith, which we cannot proclaim without reference to Judaism. Moreover, since there is a unique bond between Christianity and Judaism, revitalizing our appreciation of Jewish religious life will deepen our Christian faith. We base these convictions on ongoing scholarly research and the official statements of many Christian denominations over the past fifty years.

We are grateful for the willingness of many Jews to engage in dialogue and study with us. We welcomed it when, on September 10, 2000, Jewish scholars sponsored by the Institute of Christian and Jewish Studies in Baltimore issued a historic declaration, *Dabru Emet: A Jewish Statement on Christians and Christianity.* This document, affirmed by notable rabbis and Jewish scholars, called on Jews to re-examine their understanding of Christianity.

Encouraged by the work of both Jewish and Christian colleagues, we offer the following ten statements for the consideration of our fellow Christians. We urge all Christians to reflect on their faith in light of these statements. For us, this is a sacred obligation.

1. God's covenant with the Jewish people endures forever.
For centuries Christians claimed that their covenant with God replaced or superseded the Jewish covenant. We renounce this claim. We believe that God does not revoke divine promises. We affirm that God is in covenant with both Jews and Christians. Tragically, the entrenched theology of supersessionism continues to influence Christian faith, worship, and practice, even though it has been repudiated by many Christian denominations and many Christians no longer accept it. Our

recognition of the abiding validity of Judaism has implications for all aspects of Christian life.

2. Jesus of Nazareth lived and died as a faithful Jew.

Christians worship the God of Israel in and through Jesus Christ. Supersessionism, however, prompted Christians over the centuries to speak of Jesus as an opponent of Judaism. This is historically incorrect. Jewish worship, ethics, and practice shaped Jesus's life and teachings. The scriptures of his people inspired and nurtured him. Christian preaching and teaching today must describe Jesus' earthly life as engaged in the ongoing Jewish quest to live out God's covenant in everyday life.

3. Ancient rivalries must not define Christian-Jewish relations today.

Although today we know Christianity and Judaism as separate religions, what became the church was a movement within the Jewish community for many decades after the ministry and resurrection of Jesus. The destruction of the Jerusalem Temple by Roman armies in the year 70 of the first century caused a crisis among the Jewish people. Various groups, including Christianity and early rabbinic Judaism, competed for leadership in the Jewish community by claiming that they were the true heirs of biblical Israel. The gospels reflect this rivalry in which the disputants exchanged various accusations. Christian charges of hypocrisy and legalism misrepresent Judaism and constitute an unworthy foundation for Christian self-understanding.

4. Judaism is a living faith, enriched by many centuries of development.

Many Christians mistakenly equate Judaism with biblical Israel. However, Judaism, like Christianity, developed new modes of belief and practice in the centuries after the destruction of the

Temple. The rabbinic tradition gave new emphasis and understanding to existing practices, such as communal prayer, study of Torah, and deeds of loving-kindness. Thus Jews could live out the covenant in a world without the Temple. Over time they developed an extensive body of interpretive literature that continues to enrich Jewish life, faith, and self-understanding. Christians cannot fully understand Judaism apart from its post-biblical development, which can also enrich and enhance Christian faith.

5. The Bible both connects and separates Jews and Christians.

Some Jews and Christians today, in the process of studying the Bible together, are discovering new ways of reading that provide a deeper appreciation of both traditions. While the two communities draw from the same biblical texts of ancient Israel, they have developed different traditions of interpretation. Christians view these texts through the lens of the New Testament, while Jews understand these scriptures through the traditions of rabbinic commentary.

Referring to the first part of the Christian Bible as the "Old Testament" can wrongly suggest that these texts are obsolete. Alternative expressions—"Hebrew Bible," "First Testament," or "Shared Testament"—although also problematic, may better express the church's renewed appreciation of the ongoing power of these scriptures for both Jews and Christians.

6. Affirming God's enduring covenant with the Jewish people has consequences for Christian understandings of salvation.

Christians meet God's saving power in the person of Jesus Christ and believe that this power is available to all people in him. Christians have therefore taught for centuries that salvation is available only through Jesus Christ. With their recent realization that God's covenant with the Jewish people is eternal, Christians can now recognize in the Jewish tradition the redemptive power of God at work. If Jews, who do not share our faith in Christ, are in a saving covenant with God, then Christians need new ways of understanding the universal significance of Christ.

7. Christians should not target Jews for conversion.

In view of our conviction that Jews are in an eternal covenant with God, we renounce missionary efforts directed at converting Jews. At the same time, we welcome opportunities for Jews and Christians to bear witness to their respective experiences of God's saving ways. Neither can properly claim to possess knowledge of God entirely or exclusively.

8. Christian worship that teaches contempt for Judaism dishonors God.

The New Testament contains passages that have frequently generated negative attitudes toward Jews and Judaism. The use of these texts in the context of worship increases the likelihood of hostility toward Jews. Christian anti-Jewish theology has also shaped worship in ways that denigrate Judaism and foster contempt for Jews. We urge church leaders to examine scripture readings, prayers, the structure of the lectionaries, preaching and hymns to remove distorted images of Judaism. A reformed Christian liturgical life would express a new relationship with Jews and thus honor God.

9. We affirm the importance of the land of Israel for the life of the Jewish people.

The land of Israel has always been of central significance to the Jewish people. However, Christian theology charged that the Jews had condemned themselves to homelessness by rejecting God's Messiah. Such supersessionism precluded any possibility for Christian understanding of Jewish attachment to the land of Israel. Christian theologians can no longer avoid this crucial issue, especially in light of the complex and persistent conflict over the land. Recognizing that both Israelis and Palestinians have the right to live in peace and security in a homeland of their own, we call for efforts that contribute to a just peace among all the peoples in the region.

10. Christians should work with Jews for the healing of the world.

For almost a century, Jews and Christians in the United States have worked together on important social issues, such as the rights of workers and civil rights. As violence and terrorism intensify in our time, we must strengthen our common efforts in the work of justice and peace to which both the prophets of Israel and Jesus summon us. These common efforts by Jews and Christians offer a vision of human solidarity and provide models of collaboration with people of other faith traditions.

APPENDIX D

Recommended Resources

Interfaith Perspectives

Beatrice Bruteau (editor), *Jesus Through Jewish Eyes: Rabbis and Scholars Engage an Ancient Brother in a New Conversation* (Maryknoll, N.Y.: Orbis Books, 2001).

Harvey Cox *Common Prayers: Faith, Family, and a Christian's Journey Through the Jewish Year* (New York: Houghton Mifflin, 2001).

Tikva Frymer-Kensky, David Novak, Peter Ochs, David Fox Sandmel, and Michael A. Signer (editors), *Christianity in Jewish Terms* (Boulder, Colo.: Westview Press, 2000).

Irving Greenberg, *For the Sake of Heaven and Earth: The New Encounter Between Judaism and Christianity* (Philadelphia: Jewish Publication Society, 2004).

Leon Klenicki and Geoffrey Wigoder, *A Dictionary of the Jewish-Christian Dialogue* (Mahwah, N.J.: Paulist Press, 1984).

John C. Merkle (editor), *Faith Transformed: Christian Encounters with Jews and Judaism* (Collegeville, Minn.: The Liturgical Press, 2003).

Aaron Milavec, *Salvation Is from the Jews: Saving Grace in Judaism and Messianic Hope in Christianity* (Collegeville, Minn.: The Liturgical Press, 2007).

Jacob Neusner, *A Rabbi Talks with Jesus* (Montreal, Canada: McGill-Queens's University Press, 2000).

John Pawlikowski, *Jesus and the Theology of Israel* (Wilmington, Del.: Michael Glazier, Inc., 1989).

David F. Sandmel, Rosann M. Catalano, and Christopher M. Leighton (editors), *Irreconcilable Differences? A Learning Resource for Jews and Christians* (Boulder, Colo.: Westview Press, 2001).

History

Donald Harman Akenson, *Saint Paul: A Skeleton Key to the Historical Jesus* (New York: Oxford University Press, 2000).

Marvin R. Wilson, *Our Father Abraham: Jewish Roots of the Christian Faith* (Grand Rapids, Mich.: William B. Eerdmans Publishing Company, 1989).

About Judaism

David S. Ariel, *What Do Jews Believe? The Spiritual Foundations of Judaism* (New York: Schocken Books, 1995).

Hayim Halevy Donin, *To Pray As a Jew: A Guide to the Prayer Book and the Synagogue Service* (New York: Basic Books, 1980).

Hayim Halevy Donin *To Be a Jew: A Guide to Jewish Observance in Contemporary Life* New York: Basic Books, 1972).

Yeschiel Eckstein, *How Firm a Foundation* (Brewster, Mass.: Paraclete Press, 1997).

Samuel G. Freedman, *Jew vs. Jew: The Struggle for the Soul of American Jewry* (New York: Touchstone, 2000).

Robert Schoen, *What I Wish My Christian Friends Knew About Judaism* (Chicago: Loyola Press, 2004).

Church Documents about Christian-Jewish Relations

"Guidelines for Catholic-Jewish Relations." National Conference of Catholic Bishops, 1967

"Notes on the Correct Way to Present Jews and Judaism in Preaching and Catechesis in the Roman Catholic Church." 1985 Vatican Commission for Religious Relations with the Jews

"Declaration of the Evangelical Lutheran Church in America to the Jewish Community." April 18, 1994
www.elca.org/ea/interfaith/jewish/declarlation.html

"Guidelines for Lutheran-Jewish Relations." 1998
www.elca.org/ea/interfaith/jewish/guidelines.html

"Talking Points: Topics in Christian-Jewish Relations." 2002
www.elca.org/ea/interfaith/jewish/talkingpoints.html

Notes

1. http://www.youtube.com/watch?v=CgASBVMyVFI

2. Samuel G. Freedman, *Jew vs. Jew: The Struggle for the Soul of American Jewry* (New York: Touchstone/Simon and Schuster, 2000).

3. For an extensive discussion about the pastoral challenges Paul faced with both Jewish and Gentile Christians, see: Daniel J. Harrington, S.J., *Paul on the Mystery of Israel* (Collegeville, Minn.: The Liturgical Press, 1992).

4. Raymond E. Brown, *The Churches the Apostles Left Behind* (Mahwah, N.J.: Paulist Press, 1984), 13–16.

5. Marcus Jastrow and S. Mendlesohn, "Bet Hillel and Bet Shammai," in *JewishEncyclopedia.com*. http://www.jewishencyclopedia.com.

6. John L. Allen, Jr., "Synod: Anglican bishop is a star of the show" posted on October 16, 2008, at National Catholic Reporter, http://ncr cafe.org/node/2200.

7. Donald Kraus, *Choosing a Bible for Worship, Teaching, Study, Preaching and Prayer* (New York: Seabury, 2006) is a great resource for figuring out which Bible to buy and just so happens to be published by my publisher!

8. Comparative translations include: Douay-Rheims Bible; Revised Standard Version Catholic Bible; New American Bible; NRSV Catholic Bible (Anglicized); Jerusalem Bible; Good News Translation; New Jerusalem Bible; and Christian Community Bible.

9. Phyllis Tickle, *The Great Emergence: How Christianity is Changing and Why* (Grand Rapids, Mich.: Baker Books, 2008) surveys what, in hindsight, appear to be predictable ruptures within Christianity and suggests that one is going on right now.

10. Piero Scaruffi, "A time-line of Christianity and Judaism," http:// www.scaruffi.com/politics/christia.html

11. http://www.jewishvirtuallibrary.org/jsource/History/rabbi.html

12. Susan Lynn Peterson, *Timeline Charts of the Western Church* (Grand Rapids, Mich.: Zondervan Publishing House, 1999), 20.

13. Pioneer groups involved with interfaith efforts include the Institute for Christian & Jewish Studies (ICJS), established in 1987, and the Christian Scholars Group on Christian-Jewish Relations, established in 1969 and now housed at the Center for Christian-Jewish Learning at Boston College.

14. Marvin R. Wilson, *Our Father Abraham: Jewish Roots of the Christian Faith* (Grand Rapids, Mich.: Eerdmans Publishing Company, 1989), 40.

15. Jacob Neusner, William Green, Ernest Frerich (eds.), *Judaisms and Their Messiahs at the Turn of the Christian Era* (Cambridge: Cambridge University Press, 1987).

16. The Shema is the prayer of all prayers for Jews: "Hear, O Israel, the Lord our God, the Lord is One."

17. David Rausch, *Building Bridges* (Chicago: Moody Press, 1988), 100.

18. Roman Catholics, Lutherans, and Anglican/Episcopalians all have catechisms, summaries of Christianity's principles, usually in a question and answer format. The term originated during the early sixteenth century. Martin Luther, who was the first to emphasize the importance of ongoing, rigorous catechesis, would probably have been appalled to have this approach to scripture study compared to Talmud Torah.

19. Donald Harman Akenson emphasizes the value to staying focused on the dominant religious parties, writing that "to focus too much on the individual groups is to miss what was going on. Most of the religious parties were like fire flies, short-lived and leaving no material record." Donald Harman Akenson, *Surpassing Wonder: The Invention of the Bible and the Talmuds* (New York: Harcourt Brace & Company, 1998), 133.

20. Donald Harman Akenson, *Saint Saul: A Skeleton Key to the Historical Jesus* (New York: Oxford University Press, 2000).

21. The Holy Ark is not synonymous with the big boat Noah built to hold a zillion animals (Genesis 6–7).

22. Friedrich Rest, *Our Christian Symbols* (Cleveland, Ohio: The Pilgrim Press, 1954), 60–62.

23. Shameless self-promotion: Meredith Gould, *The Catholic Home: Celebrations and Traditions for Holidays, Feast Days, and Every Day* (New York: Doubleday, 2004).

24. Although this Order of Service is followed by some Evangelical Protestant churches as well, not every service includes Communion.

25. Depending on the transliteration, the Hebrew word for "holy" is spelled either "kodesh" or "kodosh." I feel compelled to mention this because the correct spelling of this Hebrew transliteration seems to be an issue for some biblical scholars.

26. One reader has questioned whether the ancients would have made the connection between rain and rainbow. Probably not, but we can!

27. For summaries and discussions of this scholarship, see: Donald Harman Akenson, *Surpassing Wonder: The Invention of the Bible and the Talmuds* (New York: Harcourt Brace, 1998), 199–207; Brad H. Young, *Jesus the Jewish Theologian* (Peabody, Mass.: Hendrickson Publishers, 1995), 13–17.

28. The passage continues: ". . . so that at the name of Jesus every knee should bend, in heaven and on earth and under the earth, and every tongue should confess that Jesus Christ is Lord, to the glory of God the Father" (Philippians 2:10–11).

29. Paul Meyendorff, "Toward Mutual Recognition of Baptism" in Thomas F. Best (ed.), *Baptism Today: Understanding, Practice, Ecumenical Implications* (Collegeville, Minn.: Liturgical Press, 2008), 195–206; James F. Puglisi, "Unity in Diversity: Convergence in the Churches' Baptismal Practices" in Thomas F. Best (ed.), op. cit., 207–211; Karen B. Westerfield Tucker in Best (ed.), op. cit., 213–224.

30. Belligerent comment from one reader, "I've never seen this done." Snarky rebuttal comment from another reader, "I have." Yes, I endured such bickering throughout the process of writing this book.

31. The Sacrament of Holy Communion is also called: Eucharist, The Breaking of Bread, The Lord's Supper, and Holy Liturgy. Roman Catholics also refer to it as Holy Mass or Mass.

32. North American Jews rediscovered and revived the venerable tradition of *chavurah* toward the end of the twentieth century C.E. Within a few decades, the chavurah movement had evolved to include self-governing fellowships frequently but not necessarily affiliated with synagogues. It should come as no surprise that contemporary chavurot emerged as egalitarian communes began dotting the cultural landscape.

33. For an easy-to-understand discussion about the debate about Holy Communion between Luther and Zwingli, see: Carl E. Braaten, *Principles of Lutheran Theology, Second Edition* (Minneapolis, Minn.: Fortress Books, 2007). 117–121.

34. Roman Catholic liturgy, Preface of Sundays in Ordinary Time I.

35. *Book of Common Prayer,* Eucharistic Prayer C, 370.

36. In 2001, the Episcopal Church and the Evangelical Lutheran Church of America entered into "full communion" after thirty years of dialogue, the results of which are set forth in the document, "Called to Common Mission." The text is available online at both the ELCA and Episcopal Church websites.

37. "The Eucharist: A Lutheran-Roman Catholic Statement," October 1, 1967. http://www.usccb.org/seia/luthrc_eucharist_1968.shtml

38. In 1999, the Lutheran World Federation and the Roman Catholic Church signed the "Joint Declaration on the Doctrine of Justification."

39. Brad H. Young, *Jesus the Jewish Theologian* (Peabody, Mass.: Hendrickson Publishers, 1995), 119–125.

40. Leonard J. Doyle OblSB (trans.), *Saint Benedict's Rule for Monasteries* (Collegeville, Minn.: Order of Saint Benedict, 1948, 2001). For a contemporary interpretation of The Rule see: John McQuiston II, *Always We Begin Again: The Benedictine Way of Living* (Harrisburg, Pa.: Morehouse Publishing, 1996). If you're scripture savvy enough to notice something weird about the citation from Psalm 47, please be assured that this quote has been taken from Doyle's translation of *The Rule* and I haven't a clue which scripture translation he was using.

41. Peter Lombard, *Quatuor libri Sententiarum* (written 1147–1151). Translation in progress through "The Commentary Project." See: http://www.franciscan-archive.org/bonaventura/commentary-project. html. See also: Joseph de Ghellinck, "Peter Lombard," *The Catholic*

Encyclopedia, Vol. 11, (New York: Robert Appleton Company, 1911). http://www.newadvent.org/cathen/11768d.html

42. Martin Luther, *On the Babylonian Captivity of the Church* (1520) in *Luther's Works* (Philadelphia: Muhlenberg, 1959), vol. 36, 91–92. See also: Project Wittenberg Online: http://www.ctsfw.edu/etext/luther/ babylonian/babylonian.htm#Top

43. King Henry VIII, *The Defence of the Seven Sacraments* (1521). So enthralled was he with this attack against Luther that Pope Leo X conferred the title "Defender of the Faith" on Henry and didn't even take it back after Henry broke with Rome. *Assertio Septem Sacramentorum* or *Defence of the Seven Sacraments* (New York: Benziger Brothers, 1908).

44. *The Book of Common Prayer* (New York: Church Publishing Incorporated, certified February, 2007), 860.

45. Susan Lynn Peterson, *Timeline Charts of the Western Church* (Grand Rapids, Mich.: Zondervan Publishing House, 1999). www. scaruffi.com/politics/christia.html; www.pbs.org/wgbh/pages/frontline/ shows/religion/maps/chron.html

46. Jules Isaac, *The Teaching of Contempt: Christian Roots of Anti-Semitism* (New York: Holt, Rinehart & Winston, 1964). H. Weaver (trans.).

47. Norman A. Beck, "Replacing Barriers with Bridges" in John C. Merkle (editor), *Faith Transformed: Christian Encounters with Jews and Judaism* (Collegeville, Minn.: The Liturgical Press, 2003), 85.

48. An excerpt from the "Statement of Most Reverend Richard J. Sklba, Auxiliary Bishop of Milwaukee Chairman, United States Conference of Catholic Bishops Committee on Ecumenical and Interreligious Affairs," reads:

"The Holy Father has chosen to omit from his revision any language from the various editions of the (Latin) Missal of 1962 that have long been associated with negative images of Jews. For example, there are no references to the 'blindness of the Jews,' to the 'lifting of a veil from their heart,' or to their 'being pulled from darkness.' Pope Benedict XVI has chosen to present the relationship of the Church and the Jews within the mystery of salvation as found in Saint Paul's Letter to the Romans (cf. Rom 11:11–32). Central to the concerns of the Holy Father is the clear articulation that salvation comes through faith in Jesus Christ and his Church. It is a faith that must never be imposed but always freely chosen. The Catholic Church in the United States remains steadfastly committed to deepening its bonds of friendship and mutual understanding with the Jewish community."

http://www.usccb.org/comm/archives/2008/08-016.shtml

49. General Convention Journal of 1964, 279–280.

50. See also the document released on the tenth anniversary of Nostra Aetate: *Statement on Catholic-Jewish Relations,* National Conference of Catholic Bishops, 1975.

51. http://archive.elca.org/ecumenical/interreligious/jewish/declaration.html

52. Statement appeared as a full-page advertisement in *The New York Times*, Sunday, September 10, 2000, page 23, New England edition. Written and signed by: Tikva Freymer-Kensky, David Novak, Peter Ochs, and Michael Signer.

53. Written and signed by members of the Christian Scholars Group on Christian-Jewish Relations: Norma A. Beck; Mary C. Boys, SNJM; Rosann Catalano; Philip A. Cunningham; Celia Deutsch, NDS; Alice L. Eckardt; Eugene J. Fisher; Eva Fleischner; Deire Good; Walter Harrelson; Michael McGarry, CSP; John C. Merle; John T. Pawlikowski, OSM; Peter A. Pettit; Peter C. Phan; JeanPierre Ruiz; Franklin Sherman; Joann Spillman; John T. Townsend; Joseph Tyson; and Clark M. Williamson.

Index